Practice ~~Random~~ Intentional Acts of Kindness

...and like yourself more

By Alan S. Questel

All rights reserved ©2022 Alan S. Questel
ISBN 979-8-9865285-2-6

Praise for "Practice Intentional Acts of Kindness"

This book by Alan Questel on kindness is so very beautiful and timely. We live in unprecedented times of change, where fear and disconnection too often prevail. Read this book and become more the loving person you really want to be and help others to do and be the same!

Stephen Gilligan, Ph.D.
Psychologist and author of *The Courage to Love*

Some books come to life when they are more needed. This is one of them. A kinder world is clearly a priority right now. To have a path to do that in a funny, clever, deep and structured way, a huge gift. Alan helps you to go from the idea of kindness to the act, to go from your head to your heart. You will be guided for someone who breath and live kindness and will take you step by step to reconnect with your loving nature.

Lea Kaufman, Creator of LK Movimiento Inteligente®,
author of *Apoderate de tu Cuerpo and El Puente a la Consciencia*

Alan is a master teacher who guides students around the world to discover themselves. In a time of change and uncertainty that separates us, this is a timeless book that addresses our collective hunger for kindness and connection. With kindness we can build our capacity to work together.

Mark D Bennett, author *Uniting by Design: the Architecture of Creative Collaboration*

How do we heal a fractured world? In this book, Alan Questel makes a compelling case for a simple answer: Be kind. Alan offers an accessible and practical guide for how to bring more love, respect, and dignity to others and to ourselves. It's a timely and useful book on how to address a perennial and profound human need.

Justin Talbot Zorn, Public Policy Consultant, and Senior Adviser at the Center for Economic and Policy Research and author of *Golden: The Power of Silence in a World of Noise*

Alan Questel has written a timely book about kindness that is especially relevant in these divisive and stressful times. The author draws in the reader right from the beginning by revealing his own personal inner struggles that led him ultimately to explore the role of kindness in significantly shaping his life. He experienced the true meaning of the Dalai Lama's words, "My religion is very simple. My religion is kindness." Like many people who have positive life-changing experiences, the author had a deep desire to share what he learned with others. The book is a clearly written, practical guide that takes the reader step-by-step through the profoundly rewarding journey towards kindness toward self and others.

Erica Elliott, MD, medical doctor, speaker, and author of *Medicine and Miracles in the High Desert*

Alan Questel has written the right book at the right time. Kindness is the thing we need. Practice Intentional Acts of Kindness is a book worth reading and living. It is a useful, highly readable, practical and enlightened guide for embodying the sublime virtue-kindness. It clearly lays out how to make kindness more and more a part of one's life.

Jay Schulkin PhD, University of Washington, School of Medicine, co-author of *The Brain in Context: A pragmatic Guide to Neuroscience* and 30+ other books on neuroscience, culture and philosophy

Kindness is a way of being and a skill. It can make us healthier and happier and improve the world around us and it can be cultivated in yourself. Alan Questel takes us in this book along the path of intentional kindness. It's an exciting, moving and transformative journey.

Michael Powell, NY Times reporter and columnist, winner of the Pulitzer Prize and author of *Canyon Dreams: A Basketball Season on the Navajo Reservation*

Practice Intentional Acts of Kindness by Alan Questel is a refreshing and thorough view into what is happening when you experience kindness and how to act with more kindness. Alan is kindly guiding you through a series of valuable and interesting reflections and tasks through which you will get to know yourself better and will find more and more satisfying ways to interact with your world.

Konrad Wiesendanger, MSc. author of *ESM-Embodied Stress Management*

Alan Questel is a master teacher who beautifully integrates learning principles and diverse strategies into a practical guide for living a better life. His stories, research and exercises are engaging and relevant. This lovingly crafted exploration of kindness will open your eyes to a rich world of self-study.

Lavinia Plonka, author of *What Are You Afraid Of and others*

By nature I am allergic to self-help books. This book is an exception though, touching on a topic that could change the world if we all embraced it ...kindness. It is complete with to do lists, excellent stories, and a good dose of Alan's innate humor. Kindness, in the way that it is presented here, is a fundamental key, a breath of fresh air that indeed could make the world a better place. Most of us have had that "moment of kindness" from an unknown stranger and know how deeply it touched us. This book will do the same.

Bob Schrei, co-author of *SourcePoint Therapy: Exploring the Blueprint of Health*

I have known Alan Questel since 2004. It is inevitable that he has written a book on kindness – kindness emerges from Alan as naturally as breathing; so, when he writes these things, he writes from an embodied knowing – that word…authentic! Alan's 'way' of demonstrating kindness is funny, energetic, smart, vibrant, warm, and generous. And this is where this book makes its unique mark. As we begin to understand more and more about the human brain and its neuroplastic potential, we are coming to realize that Kindness is a well networked function of the brain that is embodied as an ACTION. It is not simply a concept or a trait, a nice thing to talk about or something to wish for or observe. Kindness is a behavior that can be learnt, enhanced, trained. Alan takes you through processes where kindness can emerge from you, you can learn to receive it and you can think it, sense it, feel it, **do it!** I highly recommend Alan and his lived experience to you.It will be an intentional act of kindness to yourself and to the world if you read this book and enact it!

Susan Hillier, Professor of Neuroscience and Rehabilitation, University of South Australia, author of over 150 peer-reviewed scientific papers.

For my brother ❤

For whom kindness always came naturally

SMALL KINDNESSES

I've been thinking about the way, when you walk

down a crowded aisle, people pull in their legs

to let you by. Or how strangers still say "bless you"

when someone sneezes, a leftover

from the Bubonic plague. "Don't die," we are saying.

And sometimes, when you spill lemons

from your grocery bag, someone else will help you

pick them up. Mostly, we don't want to harm each other.

We want to be handed our cup of coffee hot,

and to say thank you to the person handing it. To smile

at them and for them to smile back. For the waitress

to call us honey when she sets down the bowl of clam chowder,

and for the driver in the red pick-up truck to let us pass.

We have so little of each other, now. So far

from tribe and fire. Only these brief moments of exchange.

What if they are the true dwelling of the holy, these

fleeting temples we make together when we say, "Here,

have my seat," "Go ahead—you first," "I like your hat."

Danusha Laméris, *from Bonfire Opera, 2020*

"*Kindness is like snow.*
  It beautifies everything it covers."
~ Kahlil Gibran

Table of Kindness

Introduction		8
PART ONE	**THE HEART OF KINDNESS**	
Chapter One	The Possibility of Kindness — An Exploration	24
Chapter Two	Turning Kindness into a Verb	38
Chapter Three	What Others Think… Feelings of Kindness… and more…	52
PART TWO	**KINDNESS BEGINS WITH YOU**	
Chapter Four	What's So Hard?	72
Chapter Five	Self-Kindness	86
Chapter Six	It's All in How You Move	102
PART THREE	**CULTIVATING KINDNESS TOWARD OTHERS**	
Chapter Seven	Kindness… 5 minutes a day…	116
Chapter Eight	Look… and listen	124
Chapter Nine	The Twins — Generosity and Kindness…	138
PART FOUR	**GOING DEEPER WITH THE PRACTICE OF KINDNESS**	
Chapter Ten	Tough Love, A Good Thing	156
Chapter Eleven	Change Your Perspective, Change Your Life	172
	Kindness Depends on How You See Things	
Chapter Twelve	Spirituality and Kindness	188
Chapter Thirteen	You're the Author — A Guide	200
A Message from the Author		206
Appendices		210

INTRODUCTION

How can we be kinder to others and ourselves?

This book will answer this question, with an emphasis on Kindness in action. You'll also learn the many particular ways of connecting with yourself and others around kindness. Because kindness comes to life with our actions, and it's possible to create a kinder world when we do it together – with action.

You may have many views about yourself and kindness. You may already think of yourself as kind. Or you're not sure you want or need to spend time reading about kindness. Perhaps you believe you know what kindness is, and it's an issue for other people. You may even think you're not really kind in any way. I'm not promising what you read here will make you kinder. I'm presenting what to you may even sound like a radical thought — you are already inherently kind, whether you know it or see it yourself. Circumstances, experiences, or other people may have trampled on your way of expressing the kindness existing in your heart. What I know for sure is I've yet to meet someone who doesn't want more kindness in their life; and it is possible for everyone.

This book can help you remove those obstacles or misconceptions, and enlarge your sense of who you are, step by step, so you can cultivate and express your innate capacity for kindness through your actions.

The impetus to write this book came from my own personal inquiry, experiences and conversations. I'll share the story of my ongoing relationship with kindness, but before I do, I'll tell you more about how I arrived here.

I've taught the Feldenkrais Method®, a powerful, revolutionary form of movement education full-time since 1983, first as a practitioner, later as an Assistant Trainer, and since 1994 as a Trainer and Educational Director. To date, I've trained over 1000 people from 15 countries on five continents to become *Feldenkrais®* practitioners. My work has provided me the opportunity to help people from different cultures, from all walks of life, to increase their sensitivity to each other and to enhance their relationships with one another. You can read additional information on the method in the appendix at the end of this book.

I've come to have a deep appreciation and understanding for the systemic thinking that underlies the *Feldenkrais Method®* (see appendix B). This way of thinking permeated my consciousness and influenced how I thought about many things, including what repeatedly comes up for me: kindness. Over time, I felt led to ask the question: *If we are, indeed, a system where all parts (our thinking, feeling, sensing, and actions, or your emotions, actions, thoughts, spirit and body) potentially influence the other parts, as Feldenkrais states, who might we become if more kindness was added to the equation of who we are? What might the world become?*

Who are you? Who do you want to be?

Looking back, I see the seeds for this book were sown many years ago. For example: in my 20's I was an aspiring actor when I participated in a one-week, residential, creative self-growth workshop led by my acting teacher. We did one exercise that particularly surprised me, indeed, it changed my whole perspective on life. This exercise had a powerful effect that it's always stayed with me.

On the face of it, the exercise was simple. Each workshop participant was given ten small pieces of paper. We were to think of all the roles we played in our lives and in the lives of others. On the pieces of paper, we wrote down each one of those roles; one role each on one piece of paper.

It took time to come up with all my roles, but soon I had my list of ten: actor, carpenter, stepfather, friend, teacher, student, boyfriend, son, brother, jokester. Simply immersing myself in the process was interesting in itself; I had never thought about myself and who I was in the roles I enacted.

Then it became extremely interesting. Our instructions were to take our ten pieces of paper and arranged them in a particular order beginning with the role we were most willing to relinquish on top of the pile. Under that, we put the next role we were next most willing to surrender, and so on, in descending order until we came to the last one. On the last piece of paper was the role we felt wholly attached to; this was the hardest role give up.

As I started in, I found that some roles were easy to give up. And as I came closer to the end of the pile, I faced some difficult choices.

The role I finally put at the end was one that surprised me; the role was "friend."

This exercise revealed so many things to me. In asking me to choose between all of the different aspects of who I was, it revealed there were roles I didn't want to play. I discovered various roles may come and go however, the most important, enduring and gratifying role for me was a surprise. The role I truly wanted to play, the role I never wanted to let go of, no matter what life presented: Friend.

From that day onward, I resolved to be the best friend I could be.

Though it may sound simple, as time went on, I discovered it wasn't an easy task. I thought I was a good friend to others and I thought I had good friends. Sure, at least I thought so. There were times I found I didn't know how to be a friend, and I did lose a few friends.

At first being a true, good friend appeared obvious, perhaps easy; yet, it was more challenging than I ever anticipated.

What does it mean, being a friend?

As I look back, I can see how my idea of friendship changed and evolved over the years. Perhaps your views of friendship have transformed as well.

Growing up in New York City and later as adult I learned a friend wasn't something one came by easily. Friends were chosen carefully, and friendships developed slowly over time. Sure, you could be friend-ly with a lot of people. Being a real friend meant something else to me. A real friend was special, held a sense of trust, was someone with whom I was able to be vulnerable without fear of judgement.

As I progressed through school, life got tougher. Because I skipped fourth grade, by sixth grade I found myself in class with kids who were a year older and quite a bit bigger. Being younger and smaller, I got picked on a great deal, and real friends were hard to come by.

When I was 12, my mother became sick, additionally, she was depressed and spent most of her time in bed. To cope, I started hanging out with the tough crowd. We were all lonely and lost in some way. We spent time together, but it didn't feel like real friendship.

With what I know now, I was looking for connection, as were the other individuals in the group. I was 19 when I had my first best friend. It was wonderful. I finally felt a sense of ongoing connection! We'd hang out together and have long, deep conversations into the night. I discovered I loved conversations that went beyond the expected or superficial; these conversations took me into the unknown where I discovered things about myself and the world. This became my new image of friendship.

Perhaps because I'd missed out on friendship so much as a kid, it became extremely important to me later in life. Back when I was a kid if someone asked me, "What would you like to be when you grow up?" I would tell them the usual things—president, doctor, playboy (yes, I really said this). When I was an adult, I would tell them a "professional friend." They always asked, "What is that?" and I would explain what it meant to me:

Friendship to me meant meaningful moments of connection, including 'deep' conversations and interactions that took me past my usual sense of myself and into the realm of greater possibilities. I had a vision of how friendship looked. I would invite people to fun, interesting events and vacations. When we went to restaurants, I'd pick up the check, and paid for it all. "I want to be the best possible friend," I said.

"Nice idea," people said when I shared this and then they would ask, "How do you make a living doing that?"

That wasn't the point for me, though. I knew it was unrealistic. I wasn't able to provide everything I imagined (although I did pick up the check much of the time). At the heart of it I was looking to have an increase in occasions that fed my sense of what it meant to be a friend and to embrace opportunities to feel a connectedness with other people.

Eventually, I took my convictions about the importance of friendship into my professional life. I became the person who was available for people to talk to, confide in, and connect with. I discovered I had a gift for adapting to others' sensibilities, especially their senses of humor. It appeared my goal of being a professional friend was working — or so I thought.

Within a single week several important moments changed my perspective. Three different clients I was seeing in my private practice referred to me as "their friend." This made me pause. I didn't think of them as 'friends.' They were clients, who paid me for my time. Yes, I listened to them, counseled them at times to help them feel connected to another person. We didn't "hang out", though. Still, from their perspective, I was giving them something that made them feel we were friends.

Clearly, we had different perspectives about our relationship; it was time I re-evaluated what was happening.

I realized I needed to refine my idea of friendship, to continue my investigation into what it meant to be a friend. To begin, I looked at friendship from the point of view of actions and values, from the perspective of both giving and receiving. Importantly, I contemplated this as a friend to others and as a friend to myself. I searched for the actions, traits, and values which were essential, consistent, and needed.

Remember the sorting exercise in the acting class I wrote about earlier? If I had done something similar to discover the trait displaying utmost importance and had maximum value to me, the word "kindness" would be on that last piece of paper. Kindness is the trait I strove to bring to every aspect of my life, and the quality I most hoped others saw in me.

Eventually, I learned to establish boundaries to ensure people, especially clients, were not confused about our relationship.

Kindness is action

In a way, this surprised me. I always considered myself kind... in a general sort of way. I had never thought of it as something I needed to develop further. Then the unforeseen happened, and I learned about kindness in action.

A huge and unexpected shock happened in my family. My father ran out of money in his late 70's. He was the family breadwinner his entire life, although he had financial ups and downs over the years, I was unable to imagine his complete loss of money.

Fortunately, my brother and I were able to help. Honestly, I was not happy about it. I was never close to my father. He was an absent dad who, although not mean, was neither expressive or approachable. This trait was fairly typical for men of his generation, the 1950's dads who were influenced by the Great Depression.

This wasn't the order I envisioned my life taking. I wasn't supposed to financially provide for my father. He was supposed to leave me something. Additionally, the amount of money he needed from me each month made my life a struggle. I joked he was my Porsche, since leasing a nice Porsche Carrera equated what I gave him every month. (It helped to have a sense a humor.)

The entire situation felt like a burden and undeserved misfortune. In retrospect, I was lucky… very lucky. Over time I saw with appreciation this act of giving to my father, helping him, had brought forth something in me which may not have emerged otherwise. An altruistic action enabled me to express my innate kindness and showed me it did this for my brother, as well.

I had to dig deep into myself to tap into a hidden reservoir of generosity that existed in me. And because of that digging deeper, I appreciated and recognized how capable I was for more kindness than I had ever imagined; **and** it felt amazing!

This opening up to kindness was a particularly significant event of my life; consequently, it set me on a path to understand how kindness is an action.

I began exploring ways to continue deepening and expanding my own capacity for kindness. Over time, it brought me to writing this book, bringing together my deeply held values, my life experiences, along with my professional knowledge and training to share my insights with you. My deepest desire is to use what I've learned and experienced to guide you in ways to help yourself and help the world become a kinder, more connected place.

Every time you act with kindness toward another, you are (both) recognizing the fact we are all human beings moving together for a common good.

The Indian sage Ramana Maharshi, a great teacher of self-inquiry and self-awareness speaks directly to this.

Questioner: How should we treat others?

Ramana Maharshi: There are no others.

Kindness is an all-encompassing attitude toward the world, a stance which says each and every act of kindness influences the world.

I believe we all have a longing to express kindness. Acting with kindness is how we get in touch with it.

Giving ourselves permission to express it, as I did with my father, is an important step.

Kindness... in action encompasses compassion, empathy, concern, consideration, sympathy and care. The ability to utilize these values so they can become part of your daily actions and interactions is where you are headed.

Why is the emphasis here on action? Why are our acts so important?

We grow and change through what we do. We discover who we are, what we want, what we're capable of. We may want to live in a kinder world. We may sense a kinder world is possible and yet merely wishing (or complaining) about issues will not change a thing. Change only happens when we act on our wishes to bring them about.

This next statement deeply resonates with me: *If you want something you have never had before… you will have to do things you haven't done before.* There is profound wisdom in this statement.

A big learning came to me as a *Feldenkrais®* Trainer. As a Trainer I conversed on various occasions with a wide spectrum of differing practitioners, both new graduates and those who were in practice for a while. Frequently these conversations followed a similar pattern, which went something like this:

A practitioner will say, "My practice isn't what I would like it to be."

I respond by asking questions to see if we can pinpoint the problem or obstacle. Usually at some point I will say, "Well, have you tried this?" and they will say, "No... hmmm... not yet."

"Well," I respond, "I suggest that you do that, and see how it goes."

Sometimes, that's all it takes.

But most times, the practitioner calls me back a few months later to say that they tried what I suggested, and their practice still isn't what they want. Then, we enter into another conversation until we land on something they haven't yet done, and I again suggest they see how it works.

As before, that may be all it takes. More often though, they will call again some months later, still looking for their practice to be something it isn't yet.

The conversation continues the same way until I finally suggest they do something, and they say, "Oh, I'm not comfortable doing that."

Having had many of these conversations over the years, I can say with assurance that it's those who are willing to do things that make them uncomfortable whose practices, and often lives, become more of what they hoped for.

Interestingly, those who are not willing to do things which feel uncomfortable to them, experience their practices continuing as they were; yet, they continue to wish for more without their desired change happening.

You may wonder what this story has to do with being kinder. I tell this story as encouragement and reassurance because it's possible that some of the things you are asked to do in this book may make you uncomfortable. Learning to be kinder is possible for anyone, even when the process may not always be easy or comfortable. The questions you are asked to consider in the book can lead you to being kind, particularly in ways you don't usually think about. If you feel uncomfortable, rely on your desire to have more kindness in your life as a way to sustain you. This desire will take you through your feelings; and you'll find within yourself an ability to do the things you have not done before.

We will also examine this specific relationship between your actions and feelings to better understand how you can practice and include them as part of your journey towards greater acts of kindness.

Now, consider "If you want something you have never had before… you will have to do things you haven't done before."

Meaning if you want to be kinder and live in a kinder world, the one important thing you can do is act on it; do the things suggested here, take the first step towards finding more kindness — then, continue to the next one, then on to next. Kindness is not a constant state. It is a constant process which is continually developing in accordance with life's ebb and flow. Kindness is a skill; a way of being and acting you can develop and practice daily.

Kindness is an intention to be fulfilled… again and again and again… through your actions.

The Cherry on Top: Liking Yourself More

The subtitle of this book is *Like Yourself More.*

Let me tell you about how this came to be central to this book.

Many years ago, I put together a workshop called "Uncommon Sensing: Moving Beyond Self-Image." This was an important workshop dealing with our self-image and how we define ourselves. Countless times, our self-image is based on how others see us, rather than on who we truly are.

As I was preparing for this workshop, I was suddenly struck by the thought that our self-image is a reflection of how much we like ourselves. How we feel about ourselves tells us something about our self-image. To clarify: if you like yourself, you'll likely have a good self-image, and if you don't like yourself, you won't have a great self-image.

The discovery of this link between self-image and liking oneself had a profound effect on me.

By then I knew from my work with others that many people struggled with liking themselves. In this vital moment, I decided helping people like themselves more was a key part of my work.

There are many ways we can approach increasing our ability to like ourselves. The way I found to be best effective and all-encompassing is through acts of kindness.

Acting with greater kindness can change how we think and feel about ourselves — in a positive way.

So, in addition to having more kindness in your life…

… do you also want to like yourself more?

My guess is your answer is yes. If you act on the suggestions in this book, in addition to creating more kindness in your life and the world, you can also move towards liking yourself more!

USING THE BOOK

This book is organized to take you through steps to broaden and deepen your understanding of what kindness is. It will show you ways to embrace kindness in your everyday life. And provide you with the means to be kinder and generate more kindness towards yourself and others.

• **Part One, The Heart of Kindness** lays the groundwork to prepare you to act with more kindness toward others and yourself.

• **Part Two, Kindness Begins with You**, we dig into an aspect of kindness most of us find the most challenging: acting kindlier towards ourselves.

• **Part Three, Cultivating Kindness Toward Others** makes our desire to act toward others with greater kindness tangible and real, through specific actions.

• **Part Four, Going Deeper with the Practice of Kindness**, we explore some of the subtler and deeper aspects of kindness in action.

Each part is comprised of three chapters. Each chapter, in turn, explores a different facet of kindness. At the end of each chapter are a set of suggested exercises, and frequently, specific practices that take kindness out of the conceptual realm of our minds and turn it into action.

I believe many of us long to have kindness in our lives, and my wish is for you to explore and discover exactly how you can create even more kindness, both in your life and in the world. I present new approaches that work, often these are centered around helping free people from their habitual patterns to allow new ways and patterns of thinking, moving, and feeling to emerge.

Since your brain and nervous system naturally love learning, each chapter presents new ways of looking at kindness. You'll explore how to express your innate kindness with thoughts and processes which are gentle and firm. All of them designed to keep you centered and balanced. All of them will feel right for you and others.

The wisdom of kindness is about continuously seeking — finding — a place of dynamic balance that doesn't stray too far in any direction. This balance keeps us in a place that is *just right*.

At various points, I share parts of my own personal journey into greater kindness. This is key to all of our understandings about kindness; as one's journey into increased kindness is essentially, deeply personal. Your willingness to explore yourself and your actions in the utmost personal ways will chart your path to becoming kinder.

As I said on the first page if this introduction, reading this book will not make you kind, you are already inherently kind. Reading this book and taking actions can make you kinder. And being kinder can help you be a better friend, and it can help you like yourself more — which we all need. This book will support you in feeling a deeper connection with yourself, with others and with the world. I am confident you'll discover new capacities in yourself for moving you closer to being the person you imagine and want yourself to be.

Fortunately, kindness is spreading. In 2019, The Bedari Foundation, established by philanthropists Jennifer and Matthew C. Harris, has given $20 million to the UCLA College [https://www.college.ucla.edu/] to establish the UCLA Bedari Kindness Institute1. The institute, which is housed in the division of social sciences, supports world-class research on kindness, creates opportunities to translate research into real-world practices, and serves as a global platform to educate and communicate its findings. Among its principal goals are empowering citizens and inspiring leaders to build more humane societies.

This book is your kindness institute, a place where you do the research yourself, without waiting for research from the Bedari Kindness Institute

This book will help you break through old, unconscious, confining patterns of thought and feeling, and to free you to express all the love and kindness in your heart... you feel more connected with yourself and others.

The emphasis is not whether it's right or wrong, it's about having more choice. I suggest different things designed to show you how to become kinder and generate kindness around you in greater and greater ways. Some of what I suggest will be fun while other ideas may feel a bit challenging. At every point, you choose. how you want to proceed. For example, although the steps you'll follow are presented in a specific order, you may decide to change this order. If something feels too demanding, you can go to the next chapter and come back to the difficult one later.

Since action is the key to improve and developing kindness in yourself, I encourage you to take action. Don't wait for your thoughts and feelings to lead. Choose to go in the direction of kindness and discover how your thoughts and feelings catch up — and, in time, transform.

"Kindness is always courage"

Matt Haig ~ The Humans

In some of the chapters, you'll be asked to write down certain things. One good idea is to create a 'kindness journal' by using a blank book, notebook, or pad dedicated solely to your journey. Perhaps you will choose to keep a document on your computer, phone or tablet. In the appendix is a worksheet you can utilize for all of your writings.

Please don't edit or rewrite your initial writings/entries. Leave them as you first wrote them down. This way, you can easily see and reflect on your development and progress.

Let's begin.

How to Use This Book

There are three ways to approach this book.

> a) You can choose to read it, and not do any of the suggested reflections or exercises.
>
> b) You can do some of the reflections and exercises and pass over others.
>
> c) You can enter unconditionally into the full experience —

learning, reflecting, and doing everything suggested.

My suggestion is you come whole-heartedly to the full experience in deepening your relationship to Kindness…

Whichever way you choose to go forward, you'll gain new insights and understandings; small things in your mind often leads to big shifts in your life. Of course, if something feels too hard to do, you can always come back. This is about being kind with yourself, and bringing more kindness into your life

Every idea and all the information you get here can be utilized immediately without preparation or further understanding. You don't have to be proficient before you begin. What is most important is being kind to yourself as you proceed. Go slowly and gently. Be prepared to have some successes, and some failures. Give yourself the time to take it in and let yourself feel it.

PART ONE
The Heart of Kindness

*"The very nature of kindness is to spread.
 If you are kind to others, today
they will be kind to you,
    and tomorrow to somebody else."*

~ Sri Chinmoy

CHAPTER ONE

The Possibility of Kindness -- An Exploration

How kind are you? How kind would you like to be? How kind can you be?

You picked this book up, and this means you probably have a genuine desire to be more kind. You want to live in a kinder world, and perhaps you know that creating a kinder world begins with you and with each of us.

This is a beautiful starting point.

Before embarking on this journey, you might also wonder: just how difficult — or even impossible — is a project like this? Can we actually create a kinder world? Or, is kindness something only a few are truly capable of? Can everyone learn to become kinder, or is this an unrealistic ideal?

At the heart of all these questions lies an even more essential one: Are humans born to be kind — or not? History and the daily news tell a discouraging story, although the truth can be even more surprising.

When you think of kindness, does a particular person come to mind? Perhaps you think of a friend or relative or teacher. Or maybe you think of someone who stands for a particular cause or ideology, such as the Dali Lama, Mother Teresa, Gandhi or Jesus. Regardless of who comes to mind, you might think it's likely they weren't born that way. Or consider, maybe they were. Maybe we all are!

In their article, "The Moral of Babies" *(The New York Times Magazine, May 5, 2010)*, authors Paul Bloom and Karen Wynn write,

"A growing body of evidence . . . suggests that humans do have a rudimentary moral sense from the very start of life. With the help of well-designed experiments, you can see glimmers of moral thought, moral judgment and moral feeling even in the first year of life." [1]

The researchers go on to say,

"Since natural selection works, at least in part, at a genetic level, there is a logic to being instinctively kind to our kin, whose survival and well-being promote the spread of our genes."[1]

They conclude with:

"Babies possess certain moral foundations — the capacity and willingness to judge the actions of others, some sense of justice, gut responses to altruism and nastiness. Regardless of how smart we are, if we didn't start with this basic apparatus, we would be nothing more than amoral agents, ruthlessly driven to pursue our self-interest. But capacities as babies are sharply limited. It is the insights of rational individuals that make a truly universal and unselfish morality something that our species can aspire to."[1]

While you might have thought that many of us weren't "born this way," it seems as infants, all of us have a predisposition towards altruism and the ability to discern un-kind behavior.

We all have the capacity for kindness; however, for it to grow and show up in our actions this innate predilection needs nurturing to develop it fully. Ideally, our families and sociocultural environments foster kindness toward others and self. Even if these fall short, we each have the ability at any time to take responsibility for developing our capacity for kindness — continuously and consciously — throughout our lives.

In other words, kindness is a skill. Developing and cultivating it is a process and journey over a lifetime, there is no final destination.

The challenges that life brings us hones and tests our capacity for kindness. The real telling is whether we are able to remain kind in challenging circumstances.

Everyone faces difficult moments in his or her life. Everyone makes mistakes. This is not what is important. What's important is how we respond. *We have the ability to be kind and become kinder.*

You will learn in the course of this book that developing your capacity for kindness often requires changing your relationships… first, with yourself, then with your relationship with others.

Change is not always easy. It will require courage on your part to tolerate the feelings that are at times uncomfortable.

It is possible changes in your capacity for kindness will show up in a big way, and can be dramatic. It is likely your shifts towards more kindness will happen slowly, with little hints of it emerging over time, in steps. One doesn't typically become kind all at once. Patience is key to your development. And you'll know when it's working.

How do you begin to cultivate more kindness?

You may think your first step is to set goals and identify how and in what ways you'll be kinder. The opposite is true. The first step is to recognize how and in what ways *you are already kind*. To tap into the ways you're *already kind and appreciate* the fact your desire to be kinder comes from what's already present in your life. Knowing about where you begin will also provide you with more insight into where you want to go.

Your first step to creating and living in a kinder world... being kinder with yourself and others...

Identify your baseline, and next, set your intentions, and shift your perspective

Answer the questions in each section. Allow time to explore them. 20-40 minutes is a good start

- Do the best you can with each question, answering as completely as possible. Don't worry if you forget something. You can always come back and add to your answers. Just do not change or erase anything you initially write.

- For now, write your answers to each question on a separate page of its own. You'll look at connecting them later on.

- If you use the worksheet provided at the back of the book and downloadable from my website www.practicing-kindness.com/worksheet, you will see additional columns. Leave them blank, you'll utilize them later.

Your baseline, or starting place, will provide a frame of reference.

1. ***Whom are you already kind towards?***

    Remember, you are kind whether you see it or not, and you are already demonstrating your kindness in many ways. Take a moment to think about it and make a list.

    In your answer, include people, animals, plants, insects, groups that you participate in, plus causes and/or nonprofits you support and you can include yourself on this list.

    Take your time with your list. Once you feel it's relatively complete, continue to question #2.

2. ***How do you demonstrate this kindness?***

    Identify the many different ways you demonstrate kindness. For example, how do you let someone know you're feeling kindly towards him or her? How do you communicate kindness toward an animal, or toward a group or organization? Is it by giving them your attention, taking certain actions, performing tasks or how you speak to them?

It's important to list every method of kindness you undertake. Again, take your time until you feel satisfied with what you wrote. Great! Now let's unpack what you wrote, beginning with the first question Who are you already kind towards?

How do you feel about what you wrote?

Are you happy with your list?

Did anything about it surprise you? What was it?

Did you leave out a name or two that you would like include? Add them to your list now.

Look at your answers to the second question: How do you demonstrate that kindness?

Was it easy or difficult for you to identify all the many ways you show kindness?

Did thinking about this spark even more ideas about how you might demonstrate kindness beyond what you already do?

Did you only consider big acts, or did you include the little things, like holding the door open or saying, "Thank you"?

These lists represent your baseline or starting place and provide a frame of reference. Periodically returning to this reference point will help you evaluate your progress toward developing a new relationship with kindness. This baseline will give you an enhanced perspective over time.

Your Intentions, or what you want to create more of in your life.

The next set of questions will help you get clearer. This may be how you thought you would begin this process, but you needed your baseline first.

3. Whom would you like to act kindlier towards?

You're expanding your sense of possibility here. List others you'd like to act kindlier towards; yet, haven't to date.

Again, include any animals, groups and/or causes, n addition to people. If you didn't include yourself in your answer to the first question, make sure you include yourself now.

Take the time you need to reflect on this list before you go the next one.

4. How would you demonstrate kindness towards those on this list?

When you imagine acting kindlier toward those on your list in #3, what does that look like? What actions are you willing to take?

Be specific with your answers. If possible, include not only the actions you might take, include the frequency and duration of those actions, as well as the places where those actions can take place. In other words, include any details to help you create an explicit vision of what you want to do. For example, you may want to:

- Call someone you know. Maybe it's someone who is going through a difficult time, or someone with whom you haven't spoken to in a while. It may be someone you know who wants to hear from you.

- For no reason except to be kind, offer to do a chore for a friend. Help them fold the laundry, or drive them somewhere, or run an errand. Anything that may help them out.
- Brush your cat or dog regularly, once a week.
- Volunteer at your church, mosque or place of worship, at a food kitchen, or at your favorite charity.

When you're finished, pause and consider whether there is anything else you can add.

Now, let's look at your answers.

When you considered the question 3 (Whom do you want to act kindlier towards?), did anyone come immediately to mind?

If so, was that person already on your first list?

Was it someone you want to act even more kindly towards? Or did you only think of people you have yet to act kindly towards?

Did a new relationship or an older one come to mind?

Regarding question 4 (How would you demonstrate this kindness?), was it hard to come up with ways to show kindness? Are you willing to take the chance to say how you really want to act?

These second two lists express your Intentions, what you want to create more of in your life. Intentions are an important part of this process; they are not the same as goals. Goals are things achieved in the future. Intentions remind us how we desire to live our lives in each and every moment.

My intention is to help you create the kindness you desire in your life, and for you to find more of the connection you're looking for with yourself and others. Another intention I have for this process is helping you discover many more and different ways to create ongoing kindness in the world beyond yourself. As I mentioned previously, this is a kindness journey, a continuing process of self-development, it's not a final resting place.

Take a moment to go over all four lists and add anything you feel moved to add. As you do so, resist changing or crossing anything out. Your first impulses often reveal your true feelings and are valuable. Please remember, there's no judgement here. These exercises are designed for gaining awareness and setting intentions.

Shifting Your Perspective

It's time to think a little differently.

5. *Whom can you never imagine acting kindly towards?*

Now take the circle of possibility even wider. Are there others to whom you can never in your entire life imagine acting kindly towards? Make a list.

Be brave. Include the names of all the "absolutely not, no way, not a chance in the world" people and organizations you can come up with. Don't worry, you're not going to have to act on this list in any way, unless you choose to. Yet, this list is important. It helps you expand the range of what is actually possible. It may also help give you a sense of perspective when you look back at it later.

Let's reflect a bit

Look at your answers to questions #1 (Whom are you already kind towards?) and question #3 (Whom would you like to act kindlier towards?).

Are the two lists about the same length? Or is one much longer than the other?

Did you include yourself on both lists, or on only one…or neither?

It's important and interesting how we can interpret the lengths of each list. If you have more answers on question #1 (Whom are already kind towards?), then it's possible developing more kindness is necessary in only a few areas.

If your list in question #3 (Whom would you like to act kindlier towards?) is longer, you may imagine that you have a lot of work to do, and you may think it's going to be hard going. Or it could simply be a reflection of how much kindness you want to demonstrate and create around you. Perhaps it is a short list. If it is, maybe this short list represents the hardest ones to act kindly toward. What some may perceive as a 'short list' could actually be a 'hard list'.

Most likely you fall somewhere between all these interpretations: of wanting a wider range of kindness, and/or accepting there may be difficult challenges thrown in. Either way, as you progress you will gain new perspectives through different ideas and actions. With progressive steps, you will find your responses start to shift and change.

The length of each list isn't important. Seeing them in relation to each other is to give you an idea of your kindness landscape, to see the range of kindness presently existing in your life and the degree of desire you have, or want to have, to create greater kindness around you.

Remember… Your desire to have more kindness in your life is likely the reason you bought this book. This desire is itself evidence of your capacity to create more kindness in your life.

Question #2 (How do you demonstrate this kindness?) and question #4 (How would you demonstrate this kindness?) are the same, but with a twist. One is answered in terms of what you already do, and the other in terms of what you may do.

Consider:

How do your answers compare? How different or similar are they?

Do you wish some of the behaviors on one list were possible on the other?

Are there things on one list that are absolutely unimaginable on the other?

Do you act differently when it's for real than when you are imagining kindness?

These two lists can reveal a great deal about you. For one, they reflect how you value kindness. And second, the differences between what you already do (your baseline) and what you would like to do (your intentions) help you recognize where you're starting from and the direction you're heading in.

Now look at question #5 (Whom can you never imagine acting kindly towards?).

This question can help you gain some perspective on what is truly possible for you as your endeavor to cultivate more kindness.

It's likely the answers you gave in question #3 (Whom would you like to act kindlier towards?), already presents a certain level of challenge for you. If they were not challenging, you may already be acting kindlier in their direction. In either case then, considering kindness to those on your list in question #5 (Whom could you never imagine acting kindly towards?) may seem impossible — even as a fantasy it's not even up for consideration!

Yet, despite seemingly daunting, look over your list of those you could never imagine acting kindly towards. Take some time to dwell on each as if you truly considered acting kindlier towards them. How might you go about it? (Remember, this is only an exercise, you don't have to actually do it).

We are ready for the last question:

6. Consider those whom could you never imagine acting kindly towards, and list all the things you can do to act kindly toward them.

Even if this seems impossible, play with it. You may surprise yourself with what you discover.

Our perspective determines how we see things. It precedes experience and influences the way we view and understand the world. Later on, we'll look more deeply at this idea. For now, I invite you to do a little experiment.

7. Look over all your lists once more, but do it in reverse order.

Begin with lists #5 and #6 — the lists of those whom you could never act kindly towards, how you can do it and what it will take to actually do it, still imagined.

As you read, reflect on each person, animal, group, etc. on your list. Imagine what it will look like. Include as many details as you can imagine: the actual things you can do, how it would feel, what words you may use.

It's important to take your time. Don't go too quickly.

Look at your answers to questions #3 and #4, the lists of those whom you would like to act kindlier towards and how you may go about that. Again, take your time. Thoughtfully consider everyone on your list and the actions you can take towards them,

What happened when you read your lists in this reverse order?

Did it get any easier to see yourself actually acting kindlier toward those whom, till now, you had only thought about acting kindly towards (list#3)?

Did something shift when you considered those you thought you could never act kindly towards? Does the feeling of challenge diminish? What about your sense of possibility? Did you feel it begin to expand?

Can you begin to imagine yourself having a greater capacity for kindness than you previously thought possible?

This part of the process is meant to show you what might have previously seemed beyond your reach may actually be closer than you think. This isn't about giving you the means for doing it, it's about planting the possibility in your consciousness.

As a reminder, the lists you created comprise your baseline and intentions; these will provide you with a reference point to help you gauge your progress on this journey of cultivating more kindness.

In the following chapters, you'll have the chance to reflect more on these initial lists, add to them, and move things over from your imagined list to one of things you're already doing.

I am on this journey with you. You are off to a great start!

As a reminder, the lists you created comprise your baseline and intentions; these will provide you with a reference point to help you gauge your progress on this journey of cultivating more kindness.

In the following chapters, you'll have the chance to reflect more on these initial lists, add to them, and move things over from your imagined list to one of things you're already doing.

I am on this journey with you. You are off to a great start!

"Kindness is the language which the deaf

can hear and the blind can see."

~ Mark Twain

CHAPTER TWO

Turning Kindness into a Verb

What is kindness? What does it mean to be kind? We may think we know and may think it's intuitively obvious. Yet, I find when we want to develop any new capacity within ourselves for a new or expanded way of being, as in being more kind, it helps to first have an inside-out understanding of what it is. This helps you appreciate it fully, and helps you discover what you must know to accomplish what you want.

> Right now, start with your definition of kindness. What is it?
>
> **Write it down. Complete this sentence:** *Kindness is...*
>
> **Let yourself go with it**. Don't stop until you've included any and all aspects of kindness you can imagine. Be sure to incorporate all the 'ideals' you have about what kindness is.
>
> Consider every aspect of kindness you may be capable of, and all the ways people demonstrate it.
>
> Don't read ahead. Finish writing your definition first. Sometimes it helps to let it sit and go back to it over a period of time.

It's always illuminating when thinking about things in a new way, such as kindness, to look at some of the ways the world views it, starting with a compilation of definitions (pardon the repetition):

kindness ('kīn(d)nis) noun:
- The act or the state of being kind — i.e., marked by goodness and charitable behavior, mild disposition, pleasantness, tenderness and concern for others.
- The quality of being friendly, generous, and considerate.
- The practice of being or the tendency to be sympathetic and compassionate.

- The quality of being warmhearted and considerate and humane
and sympathetic.

- The ability to behave kindly - the practice of being or the tendency to be sympathetic and compassionate.

- Tendency to be kind and forgiving.

- A kind act.

- A kind deed.

- The quality or state of being kind.

As with so many definitions, kindness, the noun, is also described through its adjective. kind (kaɪnd) adjective:

- Generous, helpful and thinking about other people's feelings.

- The state or quality of being kind, in any of its various senses, manifestation of kind feeling or disposition beneficence

- A kind act, an act of good will, as, to do a great kindness

- Of a good or benevolent nature or disposition.

- Being benevolent or charitable.

- Having a friendly or generous nature or attitude.

- Having, showing, or proceeding from benevolence.

- Indulgent, considerate, or helpful, humane.

- Being merciful, humane or compassionate

- Helpful to others or to another.

- Considerate or humane.

- Being good or nice

- Cordial, courteous.

- Pleasant, agreeable, mild.
- Being loving or amorous
- Loving, affectionate.

When you look at your lists from the previous chapter in light of these definitions, did it include a lot of the ideas from both these definitions? Did you have thoughts not expressed in these definitions?

If you'd like to add any of the ideas from the definitions here, go ahead and do it now. Share your ideas on my Facebook page and see what other people have shared.

The Action Gap

These definitions of kindness say a lot about what kindness is, which is important. They don't tell us how to express these many definitions of kindness: as in being friendly, generous, considerate, charitable, forgiving, etc. The definitions are non-specific as to what each thing looks like in the world, and generic like a New Year's resolution that doesn't get done. For this reason, it's important to keep your focus on kindness through action, what you say and do. Review and add to your lists of how this can look.

As a Feldenkrais® Trainer I help others, and myself, achieve our intentions. We do this by taking an abstract idea and making it specific, tangible, and solid in a way one can apply it in action. For example, balance. Reading or talking about balance is abstract and usually doesn't help improve one's balance. Providing experiences in which a person's balance is gently challenged; when a person has to figure out something about balance, to improve it, that is making the abstract tangible. Dr. Feldenkrais said, "We make the impossible, possible, the possible, easy, and the easy, elegant."

Our question is how do we actually do (and become) what we desire? How do we turn our desire to act kindly into how we show up in the world? This is your exploration and task.

Kindness Makes You Healthier

There's a potent story about kindness in action, and its effects on both how you feel, and your actual health!

In the book The Rabbit Effect by Dr. Kelli Harding, MD, MPH, she relates a research story that's remarkable for demonstrating the positive benefits kindness has on keeping you healthier! (warning, it wasn't kind to the rabbits).

> "New Zealand white male rabbits develop heart disease much like humans if fed a high-fat diet… Dr. Robert Nerem and his team designed a straightforward experiment using what he calls "the standard rabbit model" to show the link… As expected, the cholesterol values were all high and virtually identical to one another. The rabbits had similar genes and ate the same diet. Now they all seemed destined for a heart attack or stroke… As the last step, Dr. Nerem needed to examine the rabbits' tiny blood vessels. Looking through the microscope, he expected all the rabbits to show similar fatty deposits on the inside of their arteries. Instead, Dr. Nerem had a shock. As it turned out, there was a huge variation in the fatty deposits between the animals. One group of rabbits had 60 percent fewer deposits than the other. It made no sense."[1]

The researchers were puzzled what could cause such a huge variance in the results."

> "…the research team looked at themselves. A Canadian postdoc named Murina Levesque had recently joined the lab. Dr. Nerem remembers, "She was an unusually kind and caring individual." When it became apparent all the animals with fewer fatty deposits were under Murina's care, the team dug deeper. They noticed Murina handled the animals differently. When she fed her rabbits, she talked to them, cuddled and petted them. She didn't just pass out rabbit kibble — she gave them love."[1]

As Dr. Nerem explains,

> "She couldn't help it. It's just how she was." …It turns out the rabbits were just the introduction to a much larger story. I call it the Rabbit Effect. When it comes to our health, we've been missing some

crucial pieces: hidden factors behind what really makes us healthy. Factors like love, friendship, and dignity."[1]

This story so clearly demonstrates the biological significance of kindness in action. *How can you turn kindness into a verb!*

As the common definitions for kindness and your lists show, being kind — or affectionate or considerate or generous — can be demonstrated in many different ways. As you continue with your exploration, you'll most likely find ways you hadn't considered before. A reason for this is all the possible ways to express kindness in action are not always apparent, or accessible to us. Something gets in the way. It could be circumstances, experiences, messages, relationships, other people and/or our interpretations of these things.

Before you can turn kindness into a verb, you have to explore and understand what taking action actually entails. This means:

- Recognize what influences and provokes your actions today.
- Identify what allows or inhibits you from taking the actions you say you want.
- Determine what will enable you to take new desired actions.

Although it may not be obvious obvious, a good place to start exploring is with your self-image.

Self-image Guides Our Actions

This may or may not surprise you, our self-image has a great deal to do with how we choose to act. Think about it, the reason lies in something called "self-consistency."

In his book, Self-consistency: A Theory of Personality, Prescott Lecky writes:

"According to the theory of self-consistency, we seek those experiences which support our values, and avoid, resist, or if necessary forcibly reject those which are inconsistent with them."[2]

Consequently, self-consistency theory tells us that if someone values kindness and sees themselves as a kind person, they will tend to both demonstrate and appreciate kind behavior.

In short, we like to treat others and be treated 'in kind', (pun intended).

Put another way, if we think of ourselves as kind, it is easier to act in kind ways toward ourselves and others, and we will seek out ways to do so. Conversely, it may be concluded that if we don't already think of ourselves as kind, acting with kindness may be harder without conscious thought and intention because it's not consistent with our self-image.

Can you see how understanding more about your self-image can benefit you? To shed light on the concept... if we turn to science, the research can only tell us something about how our self-image was formed. It can't help us make a change inside ourselves about our self-image. While we might be able to shift our perspective around something that happened in the past, we can't go back into our past and actually change it. What's needed is another way of understanding our self-image we can access and use to help us become more of who we desire to be.

We act in accordance with our self-image.
~ Moshe Feldenkrais

A Closer Look at Self-Image

Self-image and action are highly interrelated. In his book, Awareness Through Movement: Easy-to-Do Health Exercises to Improve Your Posture, Vision, Imagination, and Personal Awareness, Moshe Feldenkrais talks about the four components of action. He writes,

"Our self-image consists of four components that are involved in every action: movement, sensation, feeling, and thought. The contribution of each of the components to any particular action varies, just as the persons carrying out the action vary, but each component will be present to some extent in any action."[3]

In short, we act in accordance with our self-image, and every action can be understood as some combination of these four components: thoughts, feelings, movement, and sensations. Examining ourselves through a lens of each of these distinctions can give us a clearer understanding of our self-image. With this new understanding, it's easier to create more kindness in our lives as we explore self-image below.

Each of these four distinctions holds unique meaning in how they play into who we see and think we are:

- Your *thinking* is made up of your thoughts, ideas, opinions and beliefs. Thinking is almost always experienced through language. To express your thoughts, you must first be able to identify them, then use the right words to say what they are.

- Your *feelings,* often referred to as our emotions, may or may not be connected to language. Your feelings can find expression in images, intuitions, hunches, moods, spirits, attitudes and atmosphere. They're almost always felt through your sensations.

- Your *sensations* are how your body takes in and processes information. They're called "sensations" because this is done primarily through your physical senses: what you see, hear, smell, taste and feel through your touch. They're central to how you make sense out of the world around you and shape your perceptions about the world.

Our interactions in life and with the world give rise to many sensations, thoughts and feelings, often in combination.

Often our feelings and sensations are entangled or wrapped around each other. Although the entwined relationship is an important part in our emotional life, we're usually unaware of the role our sensations play. When we encounter emotions like anger, hurt, or love; we experience a particular sensation as a knot in the stomach, a tightness in the chest, or light-headed excitement. Because we haven't been taught to identify them as separate from our feelings, they're ignored or bypassed altogether. We simply say "I felt angry" or "I feel sad." I'll explain more about this in Chapter Three.

Likewise, our thoughts and feelings continually influence one another. Thoughts and feelings can be so inter-connected our thoughts and feelings to appear as one, but they are not one.

To complicate it more, when we strongly feel something in relation to a particular situation or event — for example, jealousy — we're also experiencing a combination of sensations associated with particular thoughts. This phenomenon is important to examine more closely, especially as it pertains to how you can differentiate between thoughts, feelings and sensations.

The fourth component Dr. Feldenkrais mentions is movement.

Movement is intrinsic in everything we do. From a biological point of view, movement is necessary for survival. Even the most simple, single-cell organism needs the ability to move towards nourishment and move away from danger.

Movement links your thoughts, feelings and sensations to all your actions, and provides the information you need to move through the world. Embracing movement enhances your ability to act in the direction of creating more kindness in the world for yourself and others.

Each of these four components of self-image co-exist for every person, and they're constantly operating within you, outside your present awareness.

The relationships between our thoughts, sensations, feelings, and movement are important because they form our values. The complexity of those relationships is compounded because they're changing all the time. A shift in any one of these relationships can inform, and even change, your values. According to self-consistency theory, we tend to act in accordance with our values; hence your actions are affected.

The beautiful key to these relationships is the components are also all interconnected. This means when one aspect of you changes — let's say, how you feel — it can lead you toward a different way of acting in the world. Likewise, if you change how you act in the world, it can lead you to a different way of thinking or feeling. It works the same for each one!

Once you understand the underlying mechanisms operating inside you, the question is can you become more aware of your thoughts, feelings and sensations?

I've talked about turning kindness into a verb; making kindness something you do, having the freedom to act intentionally and doing things you haven't done before. Can you see how enormously important these questions about being aware are?

Without sufficient awareness, you may believe you are your thoughts, your feelings, or your sensations. You feel sad and begin to think is this who I am. So that "I am sad" becomes part of your self-image. When, in reality, a feeling can change in an instant. You're left thinking If I am no longer sad, who am I? Likewise, experiencing the sensations you associate with being tired, and identify those as "I am always tired." What we usually don't think about or ask ourselves, though, is "what about when I'm rested?" You can't see that a sensation is not a permanent part of who you are.

Hopefully, it's clear now how your thoughts, feelings, and sensations may describe how you are at a particular moment, and at the same time, are often ephemeral; Taking action is different; once you take action, whatever you feel or think becomes something done in the world, definitively observable by yourself and others.

Actions are differentiated from thoughts, feelings and sensations for a reason. Commonly, when people want to act differently — in this case, act in more kindly ways — they wait for different thoughts or feelings to show up before making any changes. Occasionally, new thoughts or feelings do show up; yet, frequently it either takes too long or the actions never happen at all.

With an understanding of the influences going on inside you that affect how you interpret and respond to what you experience. you're left with the vital and important ability to change how you act — regardless of what you think or feel. In other words, a real demonstration of who you truly are.

It is through your actions being different that others will perceive you differently, and you will start to perceive yourself differently.

Your self-image may be habitual, yet, your habits can change. Modify your habits by taking new actions. Over time you create your new self-image.

Here comes the tricky part though it may sound easy. Change how you act before your thoughts and feelings catch up to align with your new actions. This can feel incongruent. The feeling of incongruity will, in turn, stir up thoughts and emotions that can feel disconcerting, disturbing, or irritating. Feeling uncomfortable and/or confused, you want to quit, stop your new actions. Remember, this is normal. Feeling unsettled arises whenever you challenge the status quo, or when your new actions don't match how you think or feel about a thing in the moment.

This is your current edge; you have to keep going, get past it. Move into a new place of being in the world... being more kind.

We've discussed the first step to creating and living in a kinder world... being kinder with yourself and others... here is your second step

Identifying your thoughts and feelings

At this point you will learn how to identify your thoughts, feelings and sensations, and distinguish them from each other to see how they influence your responses and reactions. This is your potential to be empowered. Distinguishing of your thoughts, feelings and sensations can lead you further into self-awareness, with enhanced self-awareness, you're able to act intentionally, this will take you closer to fulfilling your desire and stated intention of acting kindlier toward others and yourself.

Go now to the lists you made earlier in Chapter One for Baseline (question #1- Whom are you already kind towards? And question #2 - How do you demonstrate this kindness?) and your Intentions (question #3 - Whom would you like to act kindlier towards? and question #4 How would you demonstrate this kindness?).

Start with Question #1, and notice the thoughts, feelings, and/or sensations you experience occur inside as you consider each entry on your list.

There's no rush. Sometimes it's hard to identify what exactly you are experiencing, and it takes a few minutes. Start with your body. That's often easiest to identify.

Write down your observations. The worksheet in the appendix is set up for you to do this with the answers from each question.

Do this with the answers from each question.

What you write may not make a lot of sense right now. So, if there's a place where you seem unable to name what you think, feel or sense, put a star next to it as a reminder to go back and reflect on it later.

Remember, this is just the beginning. You are practicing how to identify with these aspects of yourself. There's no right way or wrong way to do it. You're already on your way to awareness and success to being more kind simply by having the willingness to begin and do it.

Three things in human life are important:

the first is to **be kind;**

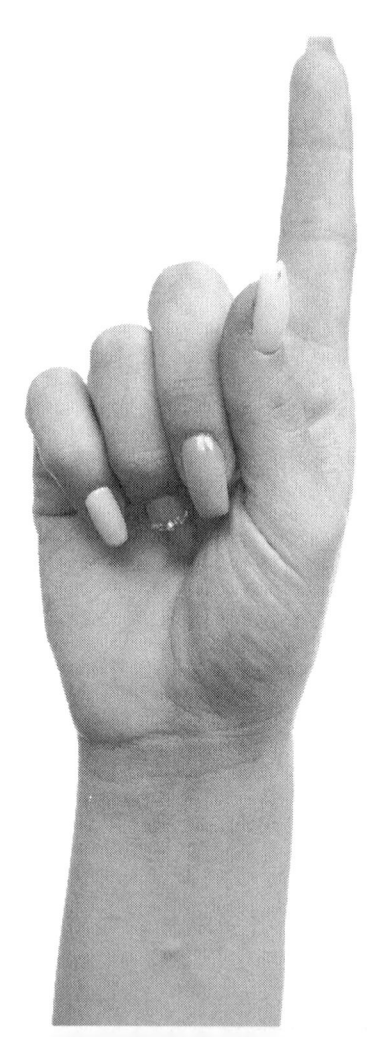

*and the third is to **be kind.***
~ Henry James

*the second is to **be kind;***

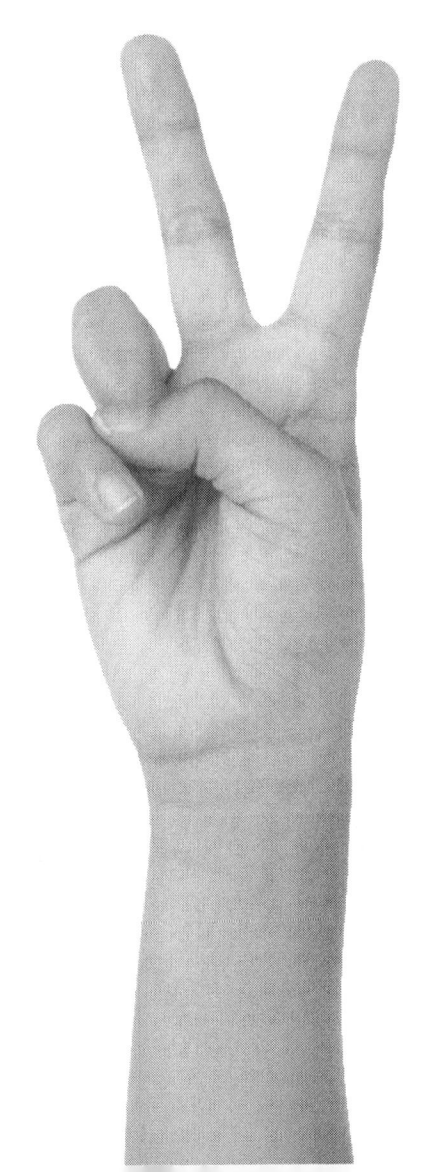

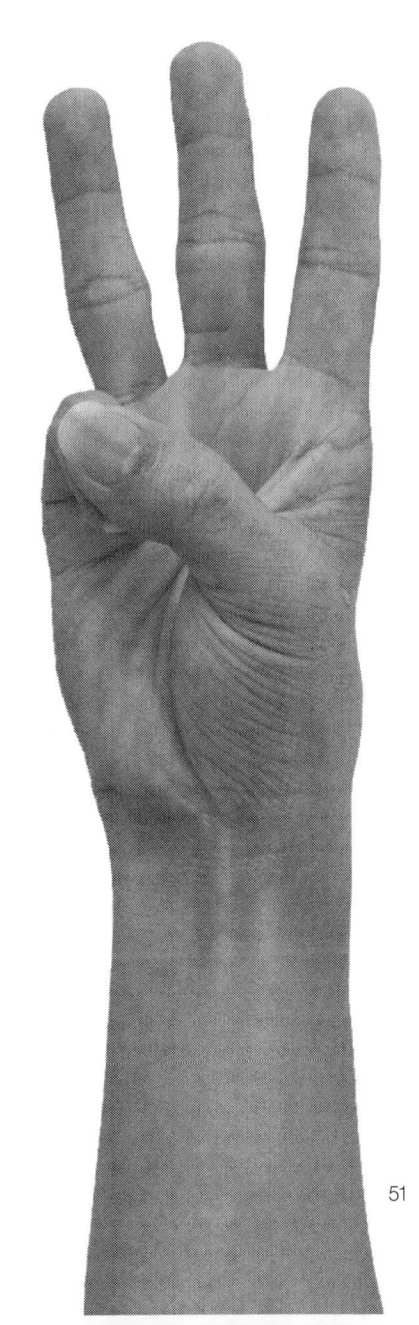

CHAPTER THREE

What Others Think... Feelings of Kindness... and More

Kindness is felt, like a sensation. You can hear another's words and sense their meaning. You can sense the tone they say them. You experience something nice that they do and know instinctually it feels kind. Because it's how someone does or says a thing that evokes that experience or feeling inside of you of having been treated kindly. For example, consider how someone can help you in such a way you feel good, or in a way you feel bad. Because you may sense their resentment or anger or impatience, even though what they're doing is assisting you in some way.

What others think

I've heard it said a person can't say of themselves, "I am humble!" That statement is only true if others say it about you.

The same is said about kindness. The premise being I may say I'm kind; yet, the real telling is if others say I am kind.

While there may be truth to this, it is also a conundrum because others' perceptions of us are frequently not accurate. You can act kindly from a place of genuine intention, and someone may not to recognize or interpret it the way you meant it. In short, they won't *attribute the quality of kindness* to your behavior.

As humans, it's natural to make attributions and have interpretations of our experience to understand or explain the reasons behind events or another's behavior. These attributions, interpretations, and inferences then influence how you interact with people. This phenomena is called "attribution theory,"[1] and was studied in the field of medicine in *Organizational Behavior in Health Care*, 2nd edition, by researchers Paul Harvey, PhD, and Mark J. Martinko, PhD, who provided good examples of how attribution works:

> "To illustrate, if a nurse observes a colleague performing a procedure incorrectly on a patient, he is likely to try to form an attributional explanation for this behavior. To be more specific, the nurse might

conclude his colleague is poorly trained, meaning the observer is attributing the behavior to insufficient skills. People also form attributions about their own behaviors and outcomes. For example, a physician might attribute her success in diagnosing a patient's rare disease to her intelligence and training, or to good luck."[2]

As these examples suggest, you can form and assign attributions of what things mean many times as you move through your day. Frequently, the attribution process is automatic and familiar, it's done subconsciously and never enters conscious thought.

Attributing your own meaning to motivations or behavior is neither right or wrong; the attribution process is important and useful in helping you make sense of things. Being aware that the process frequently relies on guessing is essential; as is understanding your guesses may be products of certain systemic biases you may have and not be aware of.

The researchers, Doctors Harvey and Martinko, go on to state:
"It is important to recognize, as with all perceptions, attributions are not always an accurate reflection of reality! We can probably all think of an instance where someone failed at a task because of his or her own actions, but erroneously blamed the failure on other people or circumstances. In fact, if we are totally honest with ourselves, we can each probably recall one or two instances where we made these false attributions ourselves."[2]

The bottom line is you don't have much control over how you are perceived by others or the attributions they make about your behaviors. The only thing you can control is yourself, and how you behave. Which brings us back to the premise that if you desire more kindness in your life, start with yourself. Focus on what's going on inside you and how you wish to be, rather than looking outside for answers or approval. You're best served by having a greater awareness of your own relationship with kindness, than looking to others for the measure of it.

Begin by getting in touch with your underlying motivations and intentions. You'll experience a greater congruence between how others perceive you and your intentions.

Feelings... Emotions... Sensations...

Earlier you learned about the relationship between your feelings, thoughts, sensations and movement (or actions) in the world. In some cultures, a good deal of value is placed on feelings, and feelings can be interpreted as the totality of an experience. I have seen this in different ways in South American and Slavic countries. As a consequence, the role of thinking, sensing, interacting and acting may be forgotten or not seen as equally important.

Consequently, it can seem clear that having more kindness in your life is largely about how you want to feel, and what's important to remember is your actions have a great deal to do with generating more kindness.

To clarify the distinction, let's delve into what we will call your 'feeling life,' and how it can help in your journey towards creating more kindness.

Your 'feeling life' encompasses your feelings, emotions, and sensations. These three things are not the same, though they're connected and come under the umbrella of Emotion. It's a vast subject with a multitude of books dedicated to studying it.

It's important to understand the essence of each part of your feeling life. Here's a short summary of the difference between emotions, feelings and sensations, based on Wiki pages:

- Emotions arise from our experiences, though we're not always conscious of them. Emotions are universal.

- Feelings, on the other hand, are the subjective representation of emotions. Feelings are private to the individual experiencing them.

- Sensations come from our somatosensory (body sensations) experience. Sensations might elicit feelings and/or emotions.

The Confusion in Language

We use words to describe to others, and ourselves, what's going on inside us, yet words don't accurately convey what's happening. Words are our available stand-ins. Which is part of the problem in understanding what we're actually experiencing—emotion, feeling, or sensation.

We often lack the clarity about what we really want to express. We use words such as 'feel' or 'sense' in ways that are actually confusing. For example, it's not a feeling when someone says, "I feel like you are not listening to me." This is an observation or a thought about what is happening, yet, when it is couched in the language of 'feeling,' it can blur the intention of what's said. Enhanced communication happens when you say, "I don't think you are listening to me and I feel…hurt…scared…angry…etc. when that happens."

Another example is "I sense you don't want to come to the party with me." The use of the word 'sense' here sends a message that's hard to interpret. When used in this way, the words can lead to misunderstandings and confusion about how the listener responds, and can leave the listener feeling manipulated. Good communication begins with a question to find out: "Do you want to come to the party with me?" Making a statement is another choice, "I really want you came to the party with me if you can."

Another part of the conundrum is the way language is used in describing experience. For example, a general tendency is referring to different experiences as feelings, using statements such as "I feel angry," or "I feel bent out of shape," or "I feel like I'm lost," or "I feel hot." In actuality, what's occurring are three entirely different aspects of feeling life! These include - a universal emotion, a specific feeling unique to the person, and/or a physical sensation.

"I feel angry" most likely refers to a universal emotion. "I feel bent out of shape" describes a subjective experience of an emotion, as does saying "I feel lost." "I feel hot" is a way of describing a current sensation.

In each case, the phrase "I feel . . ." is used; which causes confusion in communications between individuals. A statement like "I feel heavy" can become even more complex. Does it mean sad, or a sense of weight from eating too much, or simply tired? A specific word used to describe your feeling, versus the physical sensation you experience, is an appropriate method to clarify the situation.

In his book, *Nonviolent Communication: A Language of Life,* Marshall Rosenberg makes yet another distinction:

> "A common confusion, generated by the English language, is our use of the word feel without actually expressing a feeling. For example, in the sentence, "I feel I didn't get a fair deal," the words I feel could be more accurately replaced with I think."[3]

Clearly language can be problematic. At the same time, language is alive and continually changing. Shakespeare offers a great example. He experimented with spelling his name in a number of different ways, *Shakespere, Shakespear, Shakspeare, Shackspeare, Shakspere* [4].

The meaning of a word can also develop over time. Here is the evolution of the word *nice*, from the website MENTAL FLOSS (https://www.mentalfloss.com/article/61876/11-words-meanings-have-changed-drastically-over-time):

> "A few centuries ago if a gentleman called a lady "nice," she might not know whether to flutter her fan or slap his face. Nice entered English via Anglo-Norman from classical Latin nescius, meaning ignorant. Then it wandered off every which way. From the 1300s through 1600s it meant silly, foolish, or ignorant. During that same time period, though, it was used with these unrelated or even contradictory meanings:
>
> Showy and ostentatious, or elegant and refined
> Particular in matters of reputation or conduct; or wanton, dissolute, lascivious
> Cowardly, unmanly, effeminate
> Slothful, lazy, sluggish
> Not obvious, difficult to decide, intricate.

By the 1500s, "nice" came to mean meticulous, attentive, sharp, making precise distinctions. By the 18th century, it acquired its current (and rather bland) meaning of agreeable and pleasant, but other meanings hung on, just to keep things interesting."

Also, in our current technological age, an exponential number of new words are continually added to the lexicon: technology, social networking, the internet, and texting are a few examples. This has changed how we use language, how we spell words, and includes the creation of new words to express complex thoughts in brief ways.

We use language to communicate and to understand others and ourselves better. In the emotional context, it can increase our ability to accurately and skillfully use language to help describe our emotions and what we are experiencing.

With the complexity and potential for confusion in different languages, each with their own set of rules and meanings for words; it is amazing that we humans share the ability to make connections. As we see patterns we develop metaphors and similes to assist our mutual understanding.

When acting with more kindness perhaps it's not necessary to change how you use the word feeling to describe an emotion, a sensation, a subjective internal state, or an attitude. Your actions will clearly illuminate the make-up of the experience you describe and will give you more freedom to be understood. Yet, knowing how confusion can arise will help you become more clear in your communications.

Untangling Emotions, Feelings and Sensations: Do you ever have a feeling without a sensation?

Although emotions are thought to be universal, there appears to be no agreement by researchers and doctors on what they are. In her book *Walking Your Talk*[5], Lavinia Plonka refers to the lists of six basic, primal reactions identified by writers and psychologists Paul Ekman and Susana Bloch. Ekman labels them as disgust, anger, fear, happiness, sadness and surprise. Bloch labels them as tenderness, anger, fear, joy, sadness and eroticism/lust. You'll notice the lists, while similar, do not exactly correspond with each other. This is not uncommon in the study of emotions and emotional states.

Adding to the confusion, others theorize there are three or four basic emotions (sad, mad, glad, scared), and all others are a permutation of those. Researchers may agree in general on what an emotion is, however, there is not a current definitive list.

In summary, emotions are universal, and feelings are our subjective experience of emotions. Next we explore how emotions and feelings are related to sensations.

We'll begin with a short thought experiment.

Imagine you're on a rollercoaster at an amusement park. You chose this ride because you love rollercoasters, and this one's famous. You paid a lot of money to be on this exact ride.

As you imagine whipping around bends, surging up and plummeting down, gripping the safety bar as hard as you can. . . you can feel your heart beating fast. Your mouth's open, and you're screaming. You're sweating. You're feeling... what? Is it excited, exhilarated, thrilled?

Now imagine you're a passenger in a car with a maniac at the wheel. He's driving recklessly over a hundred miles per hour on a narrow, curvy road. Your heart's beating so fast it feels like it will leap from your chest. You're screaming and sweating. Your knuckles are white from gripping the door handle You're feeling...what? ... Frightened, terrified, anxious?

These two completely different situations elicit the same physiological, sensory responses in your body. Yet we are experiencing completely dissimilar emotional responses. Said another way, the exact same set of sensations are provoking entirely different *emotions*. Yet we use the word 'feel' to describe both. I feel a sensation and I feel an emotion. It can be quite confusing and even misleading.

You can surmise the surrounding circumstances help determine how you feel. You can determine you decide how you feel based on the circumstances. From this perspective, *we can say a feeling/emotion is a complex of particular sensations within a particular context or setting made up of you, the place, the circumstances, others present, and what's happening.* That the context, plus the accompanying sensations, tells you what you're feeling.

Along with your feelings and emotions in the two different contexts described above are your thoughts, the language you use to describe what you're experiencing. You may be thinking what a great time you're having, or how brave you are as you careen up and down and around on the rollercoaster. In the car with the maniac, you may be paralyzed with the thought you won't get out of the car alive.

Do you see how your thoughts and feelings are influenced by sensory experience of where you are and what you're doing? That your actions in the world can make a difference in how you feel and think? It's complex, it's subtle and you simply need to consider the two examples in the thought experiment to see the interrelationships between actions, thoughts, and feelings.

The question we're left with is which comes first? Are you feeling sad because of what you're doing, or is what you're doing causing you to be sad? Sometimes you'll know the answer; and sometimes you won't.

These differing aspects of your "feeling life" are ongoing, continually occurring, and always intermingling. Call it a human condition. Because the aspects are highly interrelated, it's difficult to tease them apart. Yet, if you learn to differentiate what you're sensing, thinking, and feeling, you become freer to adopt new ways of acting and behaving in the world. An excellent reminder is knowing that despite the confusion, the key to creating kindness for yourself and others is cultivating an ongoing awareness of yourself and how these aspects (thoughts, feelings, sensations) interact inside you.

A change in one has the potential to change another, and with that, change your experience in who you are.

This systemic view of how they're all interconnected, and how changing one aspect influences the rest, empowers you. At the end of this chapter, you'll have a chance to see for yourself.

Choosing what we feel and how we respond.

Feelings exist for most people, they come and go, Sometimes lingering a long time and other times not long at all. At times feelings are intense and other times they are elusive or unclear. Many people believe we have no control over our feelings.

The way a toddler displays emotions is an interesting example. One minute a child is crying, sometimes wailing, the next moment their world is all smiles if s/he's distracted by jingling keys or a dangling toy. Naturally, every parent knows this isn't always the case, and yet, it's often enough to wonder how the child happens to go from one emotion to another so quickly and completely. Can it work the same with us adults? We can joke and say: "Perhaps it can; if the keys are to a Lexus, a Mercedes or a dream vacation house."

Many adults have learned to ignore or suppress their feelings to such a degree that they don't know what they feel, or they reject emotions and any display of emotion in themselves or others.

For some individuals, emotions are viewed in a negative light. Part of the reason for this can be cultural. I have witnessed a wide range of what is considered appropriate in different parts of the world.

Children are usually given a bit of a free reign to explore their worlds, at least initially. This can take the form of: crawling on the floor, putting things in their mouth, having free reign to touch things, looking directly at others or simply saying what they are thinking. Then, when a child reaches an age where they're socialized to interact with others; they are given a multitude of signals, messages, and rules about the proper way to behave. In many cases it takes a stringent form of: *sit still, don't fidget, don't stare at people, don't touch, don't try to make sense of things by tasting them, you can't say that to someone.* All these messages are contrary to the way they knew themselves and their place in the world when small. In so many ways, the messages are about how *not* to act.

The teachings serve to inhibit, ignore, or not respond to many of the impulses, sensations and feelings felt. Due to this type of social norms and constraints, some emotions fall into the background, and behaviors of inhibition become dominant. For instance, when you are really excited you may demonstrate more restraint than enthusiasm, when you are scared you may stifle an expression, when sad you may inhibit tears, or when unsure you may not say what you're thinking.

The result is you can feel frustrated and/or self-conscious; counter wise and equally constrictive, you may feel proud of your ability to control your emotions. Either way, this conditioning is a fundamental part of how our self-image forms and develops. As we discussed in Chapter Two self-image affects our actions.

While developing an ability to curb your instincts and manage your behavior is essential to living in society, it can also come with the loss of your ability to know what you're *feeling*.

When you're able to consider your thoughts and feelings in a way that you recognize what they are, you allow yourself to truly experience them. Through this process you discover new ways of acting in accordance with them. In turn, you'll know how to express kindness towards others and yourself, which is an excellent feature. An extremely important lesson is learning how to feel again, learning how to identify your feelings, and choosing a responsive awareness to your feelings as an adult.

Your ability to act kindly is directly linked to your clarity about what you feel and your intentions.

I'm inviting you now to take a novel approach to examining your feelings.

Note, it's tempting to jump in and try to understand exactly what you're feeling in every moment. While possibly useful, you can come up empty, with your feelings being elusive or tough to identify. Your mindset can veer off into an analytical black hole.

A good way to actively pursue a new relationship with your feelings is to simply observe them in the moment, with a twist. Observe what you might be feeling and ask if your feeling is reversible.

For example, if feeling angry, can you let go of that anger and not feel it. If feeling sad, can you feel the opposite of sad or forget the sad feeling, If feeling hurt, can you feel something different than hurt. Working with uncomfortable or unpleasant feelings makes the exercise more powerful because the feelings are easier to identify. Let's face it, who wants to give up a good feeling for something less.

Expanding upon this idea of reversibility, it may be easier to understand in relation to movement. When we know or understand how we move we can easily shift or reverse the direction of how we are moving. If you can get out of chair passing through a particular trajectory and you can return to sitting in the chair through the same trajectory, your movement is reversible. Reversibility is more than just the forward and backward pathways. It can include the ability to change the direction you are moving in. Not only can you retrace what you did, the option exists to go in more directions than the precise opposite one. You can move backwards, forwards and in many other directions easily, without additional effort. What is most important in any change of direction, is this, before you change direction you have to pause. It's that pause in movement that allows for another possibility; like stopping your car before going into reverse. Mastery over a movement comes with the ability to pause. This same idea applies to your emotional life

This simple way of examining your feelings can lead to a different relationship with what you feel in every moment. As it gets clearer it allows you to play with your attachment to your feelings. Every time you discover you can move out of a feeling, like anger, you'll feel freer in your life. You'll have many more choices as to how you might choose to respond the next time a feeling is provoked. Even discovering you can't let go of a feeling, that it's sticking with you, will give you more choices how to respond and act later on.

> Start now. Think of a situation that's been upsetting for you. Ask yourself if it's possible to not feel the way you've been feeling about it. See if by asking the question alone you can invite new insights into your awareness as to how you feel or wish to respond.

Differentiating your feelings, sensations and actions

At this point you may be left with the thought that your sensations and feelings are intrinsically bound together and this can be an unavoidable trap. However, stay with me, because it's entirely possible to differentiate your feelings from your sensations, and, yes, it's possible to differentiate your feelings from your thoughts as well.

Many years ago, in my private practice I had a client whose shoulders went into a spasm whenever she was angry. She experienced tremendous pain as a result.

The third time she came to me, I clearly saw this connection between her pain and her emotions. She was angry and she was in pain. While working with her, I carried on a conversation that surprises me to this day, because I did my best to keep her angry.

My work with her (The Feldenkrais Method) consisted of gentle movements from her shoulder through her ribs to her pelvis, creating a better quality and distribution of movement. While doing that I was rude and would cut her off when she spoke. I was careful not to go too far, though I kept her at the edge of her anger throughout most of the session. When we finished and she got up to walk around, I asked her how she felt. She told me how furious she was with me, saying I was rude and in-considerate and she shouldn't even pay for the session. I nodded and asked how her shoulders felt.

Her response was one of shock. She had no pain...even though she still felt angry!

This was a tough lesson for her; yet, by the end of the session she was clearly able to differentiate between her emotions and her sensations. In so doing, she learned pain and anger weren't always tied together. She began to experience different thoughts; initially, directed towards me her thoughts shifted from indignation to appreciation, and later led her to wonder about her capacity to have different experiences. Her time in my office opened her to greater possibilities.

While this is an extreme example, it's a telling example how it is common to conflate emotions, feelings, and sensations, and generate thoughts based on them. This is what we've been exploring; and it's especially important when the emotions are strong, because sensations and thoughts almost always accompany strong emotions. Since emotions, feeling, and sensations are intrinsically interrelated, all of them can directly affect the actions we're able to make in response to stimuli.

I've spent considerable time on feelings because kindness is frequently felt. Again, I emphasize, to express more kindness is to act differently. Acting with kindness is what you want and where you're going. Perhaps you're beginning to realize kindness is your desire and intention. Maybe it started since you began reading this book, or perhaps it was there all along.

Simply remember, acting differently will bring up diverse feelings; if you feel conflicted when this happens, take a moment to differentiate between your thoughts, your feelings, and your actions. Many of us have to learn this, including me.

For example, every day for 16 years I meditated each morning, without fail. I'd rise and sit on my cushion for 40 minutes. Most of those days if I asked myself while I was still in bed if it was time to get up and meditate, my first thought, in less than 10 seconds was most often "No." That experience taught me a valuable lesson if I listened only to my thoughts (like not wanting to get up and meditate), my feelings (such as feeling relaxed, even lazy) or my sensations (how much I enjoyed my warm bed), I would never fulfill my intention. I allowed myself to experience my thoughts, feelings and sensations, and then I chose my next action, which in this case was acting in different way.

The sports brand Nike is another example. Its motto that says, 'Just do it!' It's extreme. This motto implies ignoring your thoughts or feelings, yet, it's not a question of ignoring your thoughts or feelings; it's about cultivating your ability to recognize and acknowledge them — and choosing to act in a differentiated way.

It's the same with practicing anything. If we ask if the time is now to do it, we too often say "no". If we hesitate, we may very well miss the opportunity.

The bottom line is you have choices in how you respond to your feelings, and they're all centered in how you take action, or not.

1. You can feel a particular way and, based on those feelings, choose to take no action (which is an action in itself). This is a common response, and usually leads to you feeling more of the same or worse.

2. You can have a feeling and choose to ignore it. Which can lead you to act in a way that allows no resolution. The consequence of this choice, particularly if it's difficult emotion like anger, can also leave you feeling worse over time.

3. You can have a feeling and decide to explore your attachment to the feeling. I suggested a way to do this earlier. Ask yourself questions, two examples are: "How reversible is this feeling? Can I shift it in some way to another direction from what I'm feeling?"

4. You can exercise more differentiation in how you respond to your emotions, This is a complex response. What it means is you can feel what you feel, and then, choose to act differently from your typical response to the feeling. You are not ignoring your feelings. You are allowing yourself to consciously decide how to act. The key two words are consciously and decide. This is what we call a 'response' to the feeling versus a 'reaction' to the feeling.

Take anger… You realize you are angry: What are your choices? You may react in a familiar way, more compulsive way by striking back or retreating. However, you have a choice to act in yet another way, still having your feeling, but acting in a new way. Neither striking back nor retreating, responding in a way where you can decide what serves you best. At times this may seem incongruent to you or even to others; yet it isn't, because it's an empowered choice, not a reaction.

The third step to creating and living in a kinder world... being kinder with yourself and others...

Exploring the distinctions of kindness

Our next step in understanding these concepts comes with exploring these distinctions through the six lists you created in Chapter One.

As you move forward, I encourage you to make a note about what you're experiencing whenever you hit a spot that feels difficult or challenging. These moments will be important to refer to as you move forward.

What we're doing is building on each thing you do. The first part of this clarity process was in Chapter Two, page 49. I strongly suggest you now do it again, because you'll most likely find your responses have changed or seem clearer. Think of it as getting to know yourself better and having more choices in your life. Once this is completed, go to the next steps listed below.

1. Pull out and review your first two lists from Chapter One: Who you're already kind *towards* and kindness. Go slowly through each entry, pausing with each entry to notice the feelings and sensations that come up in your body. Notice the distinction between your emotions and the sensations you experience.
    Since these lists include those you already feel and act kindly towards, it may be easier to separate out your feelings from your sensations. If it's not easy, remember you aren't expected to be good at this. Simply asking the question will help you gain understanding.

2. When you're done with the first two lists, turn to the third list in Chapter One *(Who you would like to act kindlier towards)* and do the

same thing, pausing with each entry to notice your feelings and sensations. Notice if there are differences in your feelings and sensations than when you read the first two lists.

3. Follow the identical process for the fourth list (*How you demonstrate kindness*). Again, go slowly, and observe what feelings and sensations you can identify. Notice if different feelings arise when you think of actually doing something rather than just thinking about it?

4. Repeat the process with your fifth list *(Who could you never imagine acting kindly towards)* What feelings and sensations come up here? Are they stronger than in the previous lists? Is it harder to tolerate? Are you able to find the feelings and sensations?

Good work! **Take a short break and come back when you're ready to begin Part Two of this exercise.**

When you started, I asked you to make a note of all the places you felt difficulty or challenged while reviewing your list. Choose one of those places and consider if you can reverse this feeling in the way discussed earlier — If I feel this way (angry, sad, frustrated,) can I change the way I feel?

Take your time with it. See if you feel something start to shift, can you identify if it's feelings or sensations.

When you're ready, proceed to the next difficult or challenging place/person and do the same thing. You'll perform this process with each person/place you felt was difficult or challenging.

Some situations may feel easy to shift while others may feel impossible. Right? Be kind to yourself. There's no right or wrong here.

You're simply practicing how to notice your feelings and sensations, and what may provoke them.

> Your final step is to go through your lists one more time, and when you get to a difficult place, imagine staying with your feelings and acting in a different way - as a conscious response versus a natural reaction. For example, if you feel angry toward a person, can you imagine cooking a meal for them? Or if someone hurt your feelings and you withdrew from them, can you imagine the two of you having a conversation about their day or your day?

What's it like to hold two seemingly disparate or opposite things? Can you describe it?

You won't always be able to imagine doing these things with the feeling you have, yet, you may surprise yourself. You may discover that through imagining that you chose to act differently, your feelings start to change. You may discover, several will take less energy to change than you thought, and many may seem more possible than you thought!

Thinking, feeling, and sensing the world you inhabit includes acting in it. Amazingly, it's all continually occurring within you at the same time. When you change one thing about yourself, the others will start to change, too.

PART TWO
Kindness Begins With You

> *"To be beautiful means to be yourself.*
>
> *You don't need to be accepted by others.*
>
> *You need to accept yourself.*
>
> ~ **Thich Nhat Hanh**

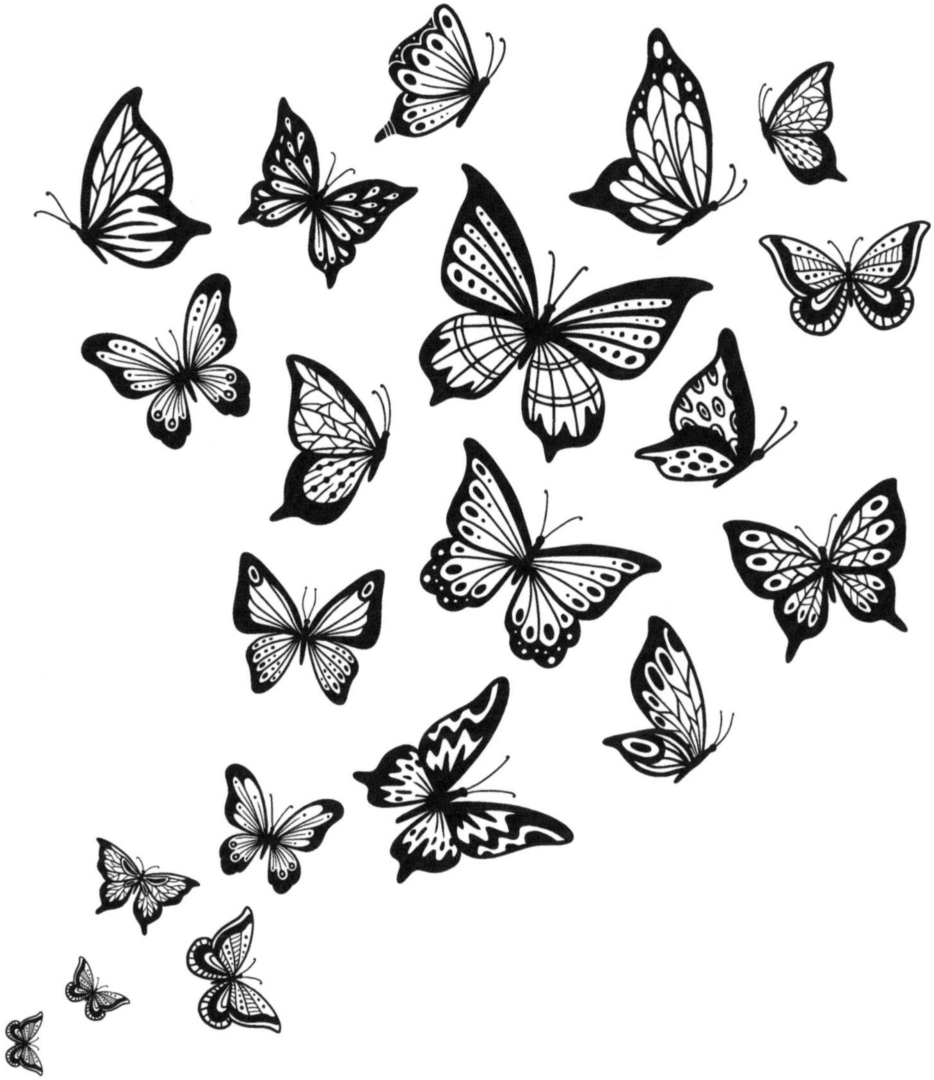

CHAPTER FOUR

What's So Hard?

In 1960, Neil Sedaka had a hit pop song "Breaking Up is Hard to Do," the refrain (being the title) repeated again and again. There was a time I thought the lyrics could just as easily say, *"Being kind is…hard to do…"*

When I first began writing this book 9 years ago, I got stuck. I believed I was pretty good at being kind to others, yet, I knew I didn't understand how to be kinder to myself, as well.

What I've learned over the years is being kind to ourselves is perhaps the biggest challenge most of us face around kindness.

It's easier to see what others need than it is to see what we need, and to act on it. Maybe this accounts for some of the delight, and even surprise, we experience when someone's kind to us. Perhaps, this is why demonstrated kindness catches us off guard, because it is unexpected.

Does this sound familiar?

Liking Ourselves More

The fact another person's kindness has an ability to surprise us speaks to something exceedingly deep in our self-perception. Remember, earlier I mentioned underlying the subtitle of this book was the concept of *liking yourself more*.

Just as I've never met someone who didn't desire additional kindness in their life, I've never met anyone who doesn't want to like themselves more. I've worked in many different places and cultures, and I've experienced how this desire to like oneself more is absolutely true for people everywhere.

When I was an actor before I became a Feldenkrais® Trainer in the Feldenkrais Method®; I had the good fortune to work with a well-known person in the avant-garde theater, Jerzy Grotowski. (He is best known through the 1981 American comedy-drama, My Dinner with Andre.) Grotowski was director of the Polish Theatre Laboratory, and I had the privilege of working with him in the United States, France, and Poland.

I hadn't seen Jerzy for several years when I was invited to a screening of a film about his more recent work. As I watched the film, I remembered his influence on me and appreciated the tremendous mentor he was to me. Additionally, I realized I had been puzzling over something for several years, something to do with my self image; later in the evening I asked him if he had time to meet with me. Although Jerzy was only in town for three days; I was about to leave for eight months of travel and Feldenkrais training; we both made time to meet over dinner the next evening.

By this time, I was deeply immersed in the Feldenkrais Method®, practicing and teaching as an Assistant Trainer. Yet, there was an aspect of my development which confused and eluded me. I told Jerzy as I was continually growing into being an experienced teacher, I understood I needed to teach in my own voice and have my own way of speaking to share knowledge and information. Yet I hadn't found it; I needed to find a teacher to guide me in my quest.

He paused, looking at me, and asked, "How did Feldenkrais find his voice?"

Immediately I answered him. "Feldenkrais found his own voice through his own infirmity. He had numerous difficulties due to his bad knees."

Jerzy responded with a *"Hmpf!"* and a nod.

This was all I needed to understand. I had the key to finding my voice! Still, I wondered, what was my infirmity? Was it my humor, which I use plenty when I teach? However, since my humor is a compulsion, it does not qualify. Was it my size? I'm not tall, at all. (Some may call me short.) No, my size wasn't it either; I believe I'm taller than I am.

As much as I wanted to know immediately, the answer eluded me. The question hovered in the background of my mind for years. Always the same…"What is my infirmity" rising up and settling down without an answer.

The puzzling question kept at me for several years until I had an astounding and astonishing realization as I explored and taught the "liking ourselves" concept. **I didn't like myself!** I realized I hadn't liked myself for most of my adult life. This had been my infirmity all along!

By the time of this realization, I'd developed enough self-knowledge to accept myself, and was moving in the direction of liking myself. Still, discovering the depth of this truth was a shock. To me, this explained why I gravitated toward teaching others how to like themselves. Subsequently, during this process, **I found my voice.**

Absolutely stunning was the knowledge the source of my pain drew me into this teaching, although I was unable to see it. Through this realization I have an understanding of the importance of working with people to help them learn to like themselves in a new variety of ways.

Today I teach in a variety of contexts (talks, professional trainings, universities, advanced trainings and public workshops), and in every one I share this idea of liking oneself more and how important it is to one's well-being. I always begin with a pause, and then a question - "Is there any one here who doesn't want to like themselves more?" The response I see most is a sort of sheepish smile on each person's face. Isn't the obvious answer "yes"? The question is more profound than the obvious, as evidenced by the woman who yelled out at a workshop, "I already like myself!" I replied, "great," and reminded her, she didn't answer the question; "Do you want to like yourself more?" She answered, "Yes".

It's a great idea, don't you think? But the minute you consider liking yourself more, the first thing you most likely think about is all the things and ways you don't like yourself. This is an incredibly tender subject; therefore, it is vital and necessary to practice being especially kind, gentle and patient with yourself as you as work on learning to like yourself.

Start with this idea - *How much you like yourself is directly related to how kind you are towards yourself.*

There's another side to liking oneself to be aware of, as well. Namely, that you can go overboard if it's misdirected as a means and goal in itself. In her article "Self-Compassion, Self-Esteem, and Well-Being" researcher Kristin D. Neff PhD writes "…while self-esteem is related to psychological well-being, the pursuit of high self-esteem can be problematic."[1]

According to Neff, "…it presents another way to feel good about oneself: self-compassion." In other words, pursuing high self-esteem is parallel to developing greater self-compassion and self-kindness.

Continuing, Neff offers a definition "Self-Kindness refers to the tendency to be caring and understanding with ourselves rather than harshly critical or judgmental."[2]

If one doesn't like oneself (which they may not be aware of, so be gentle with this idea), one can't feel worthy of self-kindness. The result can result in a harsh, critical, and judgmental attitude/demeanor towards others and themselves rather than an understanding and caring way of being. With an understanding of the link between liking oneself and kindness, one can easily see the prevalence of the human condition of Self Dislike and Unkindness.

Think of it as a loop… the more you like yourself, the kinder you are towards yourself… and the kinder you are toward yourself, the more you can like yourself.

Let's explore liking oneself more and make it personal. I'm inviting you to consider how you might come to like yourself more.

Can you immediately think of different ways?

Or is this something you haven't ever consciously considered?

For some, saying affirmations aloud can have a positive effect, so you may try repeating the affirmation *I like myself… I like myself… I like myself…*

Please note, this may not work for you. At least one study says this can actually backfire. In "Positive Self-Statements Power for Some, Peril for Others," researchers offer this cautionary note: "if people believe they are unlovable [and] repeat 'I'm a lovable person,' they may dismiss this statement and perhaps reinforce their conviction that they are unlovable"[3]

Additionally, a question worth asking is: if affirmations do have a positive effect, how long does it last? Maybe it feels good while doing it, then, it is forgotten afterwards. Do we know if it remains in the subconscious mind or not?

Try it. See what comes up.

Another question is how long must you do it for it to take hold and have a lasting effect?

As I shared, people long to like themselves more. It appears true that many, if not most, are not consciously aware of how much this motivates their behavior in both how they treat themselves and how they treat others. Additionally, there remains all the things people choose to do in an attempt to like themselves more.

I've personally observed how people pursue liking themselves more in fairly consistent ways. Often this occurs from the outside in, for example: connecting their sense of themselves to things and outcomes they desire - a new car, a clothing style, a haircut, a better job, or a different relationship.

This often comes from cultural messages and conditioning on what's supposed to make us happy. If you're happy, certainly you'll like yourself more. However true this feels for a while; the cycle can continue in endless circles when self-worth and liking oneself comes from the outside; the newness fades, the pursuit for things and outcomes starts all over again.

To be lasting, self-worth and liking yourself has to come from the inside and be an internal feeling of satisfaction that's not generated by acquiring anything. Your sense of accomplishment must come from what it means to you, not anyone else.

Note, I'm not saying a sense of accomplishment comes from making enough money to buy the things is wrong, for that is indeed a worthy accomplishment. What I'm saying is fulfilling an internal need to generate something stays with you longer. Neff writes in the article "The Role of Self-Compassion in Development: A Healthier Way to Relate to Oneself" "…self-compassionate individuals are motivated to learn and grow, but for intrinsic reasons – not because they want to garner social approval."[4]

An intrinsic sense of accomplishment comes from the feeling you did something well, and from knowing you can now do something you couldn't before. Knowing you have acquired an internal sense of yourself as opposed to acquiring something external, like belongings or a job. While you can lose your job or your belongings, this internal sense of yourself is always something you will own. It's an empowered feeling inside you of self-worth and leads to liking yourself.

If you want to see this in action, watch a child learning to do something new just because they want to learn it, not because they're made to do it. When children learn like this, they don't think about making mistakes. For them, though they don't realize it, mistakes are simply part of their learning. They don't rush to make it happen, either, because it's a process of discovery that comes with an internal reward of accomplishment. If it doesn't happen right away, they'll leave it and return to it later, experimenting and trying new ways of doing it. They'll be patient, because they have no timeline to succeed. They're fully engaged in their process, rather than focusing on the outcome. This is the heart of creativity.

For the majority of us, this approach is lost in navigating and working out our lives. We may say we are process-oriented, and it may be true to a degree. Usually, it's only the case as long as goals are achieved. Success becomes the desire rather than immersing in the process. The byproducts of focusing on the end goal instead of the process frequently results in impatience and perfection, which grow into impediments to satisfaction with oneself. Because hidden in impatience and perfection is the mistaken idea that one can excel at an endeavor before it's attempted.

I once had a student who announced with a great sense of satisfaction, "I am not going to talk about the Feldenkrais Method until I can talk about the method clearly and understandably!" For me, it was the equivalent of saying, "I am not going to get on the mountain until I know how to ski like a pro!"

This example of a person's sense of self-worth resting on external sources appears universal. A vital tool is breaking the belief that you are only likable if others like you.

Tremendously important is learning to identify and trust deep feelings of satisfaction that come from within. Another important lesson is to learn, with patience and practice, to do one thing well over time.

Can you see how much kinder it is to live this way in the world?

Impatience and perfection are blind spots in your self-image that you can't see. The beauty in this is, because they're learned, they can be unlearned.

Blind spots

Most of the shadows of this life are caused by standing in one's own sunshine.
~ Ralph Waldo Emerson

Liking yourself more and being kinder to yourself exposes you to some of your biggest blind spots. Since you don't naturally see them, it's hard to explore them. Plus, they come riddled with your unconscious history and habits. Seeing your blind spots can mean making big changes in how you live your life; if you don't know what this means it can feel scary.

When I looked up blind spot in the Google Dictionary, I found these definitions (partial):

Noun

2. An area where a person's view is obstructed. For example: *'the rear-view mirror eliminates blind spots on both sides of the car'*

2.1 An area in which a person lacks understanding or impartiality. For example: *'Ed had a blind spot where these ethical issues were concerned.'*

Definition 2.1 - an *area in which a person lacks understanding or impartiality* - is particularly relevant to you in this discussion. Although definitions tell us nothing about how you might go about unveiling your blind spots, they are useful starting points for understanding what's at play.

Looking for your blind spots is like trying to see something through a fogged-up window. You may have a sense there's something out there yet looking harder won't help you see it more clearly. Working harder or putting in more effort, the primary ways one typically goes about doing and achieving most things in life may work to some degree. Although you may have the best of intentions, this approach is usually tied to an external 'thing' that you desire to attain or achieve in your life. Directing your attention and actions toward an internal sense of satisfaction will provide a lasting reward.

The number one best way to approach and understand your blind spots is …slowly …gently … patiently …and simply.

An Oak tree is a daily reminder great things often have small beginnings.
~ Matshona Dhliwayo

When I was 19 years old, I moved out of my parent's house and rented my own apartment. Looking back, I see I hardly liked myself back then. Similar to many people, I believed if I acquired all the things I dreamt about, then happiness followed; and naturally, like myself.

Being on my own for the first time, I was suddenly faced with a dire insight; I didn't do anything well. When this realization hit me, I didn't feel good about myself, at all. My conclusion, I was already a failure, at 19!

Admitting this to myself was daunting. I felt extremely unsettled until the day I came up with an idea that serves me to this day. I made the decision to learn to do one thing well. I wasn't sure what, or where I'd start, and with some thought, I came up with a short list of criteria.

It had to be something that required I do it frequently, every day if possible, so I would get a lot of practice. It had to be something not too complicated, and be of a relatively short duration, so I can tell when I had achieved greater mastery of it. The task needs to be forgiving, so I will be able to be patient with myself, without the necessity to achieve anything immediately. I started looking.

One day it hit me, I'd never brushed my teeth well. I decided this will be the thing I'd learn to do well and improve upon each day. The good thing was I never had to tell anyone. If I didn't succeed, no one else will know. The dentist already knew, so it was truly between me and myself!

Plus, it meant I encountered myself twice a day, and each time I had to show up. Sometimes this came easily, and other times I made myself do it. I understood much later what I was doing then, I was differentiating my feelings from my actions. ... The exact thing I speak about in Chapter Three.

Before long I discovered I'd stumbled upon something that was a secret way, almost sideways, of exploring myself. Something that uniquely had to do with an internal feeling of success I generated for myself. It had absolutely nothing to do with the world outside myself or all the things I was accustomed to pursuing to make myself feel better about myself. This insight was pure revelation for me.

Incredibly, I discovered a new awareness of things about myself I'd never seen before. I watched myself create reasons not to brush my teeth or I'd want to do it for shorter periods of time. I listened to my internal conversations regarding how this practice was a waste of time. In short, I was encountering all the habits I had around avoidance. My blind spots were slowly becoming clear.

The first important fact is, I didn't stop. I kept brushing despite my internal chatter.

This revelation led to three surprising insights: First, I began to see I had these same internal conversations around other situations in my life. Shockingly, I'd been practicing not being good at what I did. I discovered, I was extremely good at not being good!

Second, there were days when I felt a growing internal sense of satisfaction, and could congratulate myself with *Hey, I am getting better at this!*

Thirdly, beyond anything, I understood I always had a choice. I wasn't subject to my habitual thoughts and patterns. I can choose to act any way I desire; despite my doubts, despite my procrastination, and despite any number of my thoughts or feelings.

I know now this feeling of choice, and doing what I did with success, would never happen if I was attached to some larger outcome outside myself. I would have tried too hard and set myself up for failure. And when I failed to achieve what I set out to do, I'd see it as confirming my negative beliefs about myself. I can hear the thought now that would've been in my head: *See Alan, you're not good at anything.*

My secret for success was I chose to work on an issue within my reach. I never told anyone about this practice; therefore, no one was able to judge me for my failures or my successes. Plus, I'd created a safe and manageable environment where my blind spots slowly emerged, and I gently and patiently learned from them. This experiment was all about me with Me, and no one else.

This next exercise presents your first opportunity to explore liking yourself more, and includes a big step towards being kinder to yourself.

The fourth step to creating and living in a kinder world... being kinder with yourself and others...

Doing one thing well

Think of a small task you do daily. Something where your world is uninterrupted and can stay intact, even if you don't do it. I chose brushing my teeth. Maybe for you it's washing the dishes, or turning the lights out when you're not in the room, or hanging your clothes up before you go to bed.

Whatever you choose, make sure the outcome associated with it isn't too big, and there's no time pressure. Keep it small for now.

Choose something you can let develop over time and keep your intention to yourself. This is between you and yourself, keep it secret for now. The reason for this is you're creating a safe learning place where you're the only one evaluating your progress.

When you begin, do it daily. Make it a regular event. Each time you do it, observe what comes up inside you — the conversations you have with yourself, the stories you tell yourself. Most importantly, go easy and be gentle with yourself. Let there be bad days and allow them. Allow good days as well. You'll discover there are great days too, and great days can be just that, great. Each time notice how you feel. Notice you're acting on this no matter how you feel about it.

To be clear here, this is not something you do for just one week and have success. Plan to do it for the **next 3 months**. This is critical. Because there has to be enough time and space for the ups and downs, and for you to patiently observe what you do as well as what happens inside you.

I recommended that you write down the things you experience.

Writing will help you remain focused and allow you to see patterns in your thoughts, feelings, and actions. You can do this daily, weekly, or at any interval you think works best for you to evaluate.

Good luck! Remember, change takes time.

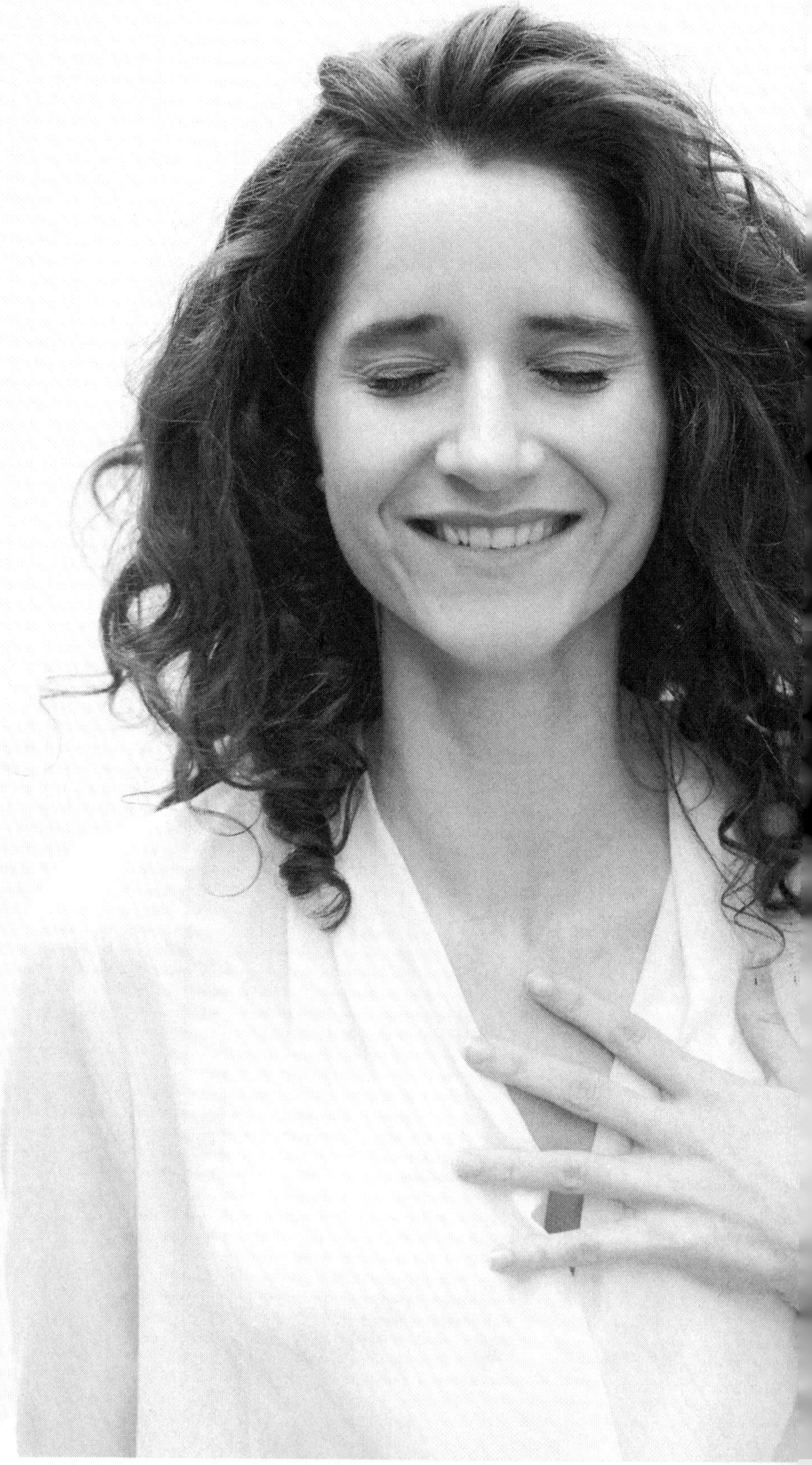

"It's not your job to like me –
it's mine."

~ Byron Katie

CHAPTER FIVE

Self-Kindness

A well-known verse in the Christian Bible is: "Love thy neighbor as thyself." Many attempt to live by this precept. Moshe Feldenkrais thought the proverbial cart may have been put before the horse in this Biblical verse. In his book, The Potent Self: A Study of Spontaneity and Compulsion (Harper and Row, 1985, Frog Books 2002), he inverts it and poses instead "Love thyself as thy neighbor".

This is an interesting idea, to turn the statement around, begging us to ask: how do we treat ourselves compared to how we treat others? There are many people who, because they display exemplary kindness, become examples to others. Oddly enough, many of these same people seem unable to be kind to themselves. Some even have difficulty receiving kindness when it is generated towards them. It may sound strange, yet if you think about it, I bet you can think of people you know who are like this.

This idea may resonate, feel familiar or be true with you. What do you think? How kind are you to yourself? I mean, really kind. Do you take care of yourself as well as you take care of others? Are you as considerate of your own feelings as you are of your family's or a friend's feelings? Do you listen to yourself as well as you listen to others?

In many ways, it's easier being kind toward someone else than it is being kind to ourselves, and it can show up in myriad ways. For example, you might easily help someone fix things around their house, yet, you neglect repairs in your own home. You might cook wonderful meals for guests and eat leftovers or fast food when alone.

The following story exemplifies this tendency I have myself around un-deservedness.

When I was in college, I got caught shoplifting (yes, it's true!). I didn't do it carelessly or randomly. I took things I needed, such as food and books for classes when I didn't have the money to buy them. One time I took a leotard I needed for a dance class. I was quite adept hiding it inside the back of my overalls and under my big, bulky winter jacket. I casually walked over to the book section, and was still hanging out, looking at books, when I glanced up and noticed two men talking close together. One of them looked at me and I remember wondering if he was the manager. I quickly looked down. When I looked up again, the man was staring at me, and I knew I should get out of here fast.

He tapped me on the shoulder just as I was leaving. "Hey, isn't there something you want to pay for?" Of course I said no and kept going. Then he grabbed me. "Come in here," he said. "I am calling security!" I immediately backed down with "Okay, okay," and he led me to the back of the store where I took out the leotard and handed it to him. He looked completely shocked. "Where's the book?" he asked.

It was in that moment I grasped what was happening. *Oh damn, he didn't actually see me steal the leotard. He thought I'd taken a book!* Now he was really angry. He'd been duped and he didn't like it. He called security. I was caught and not getting off free.

The outcome was a meeting with the dean of students who put me on disciplinary probation. This meant I'd be expelled if caught doing anything like this again. The entire situation felt horrible, yet, there was actually a much bigger outcome for me. I had to inhibit my larcenous behavior, and this knowledge presented me with uncomfortable feelings I'd never experienced before. My logic was I only stole essentials and things I needed. And now I was faced with the fact that wasn't the point of what I was doing. The real reason I took things was because I was unable to ask for things. I didn't ask because I didn't feel deserving. My way of avoiding this part of myself was to simply take, without asking. This insight was a profound discovery for me.

The upside is I saw how fortunate I was that I'd been caught and only suffered mild discipline. Although I didn't know it at the time, this marked the beginning of a long process of learning to feel worthy.

As we discussed, this concept of kindness to ourselves can translate into a reflection of our own sense of self-worth.

When attempting to discover how to be kinder toward yourself; it's important to explore self-worth, self-esteem, self-compassion, and the relationship between them.

Cultivating self-kindness through self-compassion is an essential aspect of this discussion. In "An Examination of Self-Compassion in relations to positive psychological functioning and personality traits", psychologist Kristin D. Neff writes

> "…self-compassion can be empirically differentiated from self-esteem. Although self-esteem and self-compassion are moderately correlated, self-compassion is a stronger unique (negative) predictor of social comparison, anger, need for closure, public self-consciousness, self-rumination, contingent self-worth and unstable self-worth…."[1]

Truly self-compassionate individuals don't depend on externals; for instance, needing the praise of others or needing material success to feel worthy. Self-compassionate people know they are worthy, regardless of the externals. Their sense of self-worth is not dependent of their socio-economic status, which makes their sense of self-worth a stable state. When self-compassionate individuals suffer setbacks (unemployment, not being promoted, not having much money, etc.,), their sense of self-worth doesn't diminish.

When Neff notes in "Self-compassion: Moving beyond the pitfalls of a separate self-concept", that self-compassion is a "[negative] predictor of social comparison, anger,"[2] she is saying the more self-compassion a person has, the less he or she will compare themselves unfavorably to others, second-guess themselves (self-rumination), or care about how others perceive them (public self-consciousness).

Additionally, self-compassionate people will have lower levels of anger and will be more comfortable with not having answers in ambiguous situations. They have less need for immediate closure to open-ended situations. In short, they tolerate ambiguity in life well.

Saying this in colloquial language, self-compassionate individuals cut themselves some slack. They're kinder to themselves because they know their self-worth doesn't depend upon how they perform in life and/or in front of others. They act as their own judges, and they tend not to judge themselves harshly.

Feeling this confident and sure within yourself may be a hard concept to grasp, especially when you add doing it with ease. Consider this: how often do you refuse help or support because you feel uncomfortable accepting it? Can this discomfort come from feeling you don't merit the gift or that you don't deserve it?

Your problem is you're ... too busy holding onto your unworthiness.
~ Ram Dass

For one reason or another, each of us has grown accustomed to a certain level of kindness towards ourselves. Whatever that level is, and however we reached it, it's the threshold of how much kindness we can tolerate receiving. "Tolerate" may seem like an odd choice of words, yet, it's entirely appropriate because it means how much kindness you will allow without interfering.

In filling out List #3 *(Who would you like to act more kindly towards?)* in Chapter One, did you include yourself? If not, think about it now.

In creating more kindness in your world, you serve others when you consider and accept kindness towards yourself. Because *the kinder you can be towards yourself, the kinder you can be towards others.*

The Dali Lama says it beautifully: *"If you don't love yourself, you cannot love others. You will not be able to love others. If you have no compassion for yourself then you are not able [capable] of developing compassion for others."*

Take heart. You are not alone if you have trouble being kind and/or having compassion for yourself. Researcher Neff says, "Most people say they are less nurturing and harsher with themselves than they are with other people. Self-compassionate individuals, on the other hand, say they are equally kind to themselves and others." (Neff, 2003).

It's important you set the intention to become more self-compassionate and kinder to yourself.

When you think of being kinder to yourself, what thoughts or feelings come up? Perhaps you think you're already kind to yourself and it's not something you need to change. Maybe you're not sure how to identify your thoughts and feelings around it. Try looking at it from another angle: In the best of all worlds, what would you change about how others behave towards you? What could someone else do (or do differently) to help you feel they were treating you with more kindness?

It's time to get out your notebook, again.

Make two lists.

1. *In your perfect world, how would you like others to treat you?*
   Really go for it, without judgement or second guessing what's possible. Include everything you can imagine. Be generous, be extravagant.

2. *Choose 3 or 4 people you know and consider what you want to be different in how they treat you. How could the people you know, treat you more kindly?*

How will these people act and what will they do to treat you kindlier? Again, let go of judgements and second guessing what they may do or what they are willing to do. You have no idea what someone may or may not do. Be willing to find out.

Now, see what you can do for yourself first. Then we'll see how you can ask for more kindness from others.

Look at the first list you just completed: (In your perfect world how would you like others to treat you?) As you read each entry, pause and ask, Is this something I can do for myself?

For example, if you wrote, "I would like my partner to make coffee for me in the morning." The first step is to shift it around and ask yourself, "Can I make coffee for myself every morning?" Doesn't it seem obvious? Of course, you can!

Your goal is to replace feeling a sense of lack over what you're not getting from someone else with an intentional act of doing it for yourself. You can take this a step further by starting to make coffee for your partner, hence, generating more kindness by giving to another.

With little effort you can find dozens of things you've been wanting others to do that you can do for yourself. This may include getting help cleaning the house or having someone cook a meal for you.

One of the big mistakes most of us make is waiting for someone else to help us feel better about ourselves. An effective and empowering method to increase self-worth is first acting in ways to give ourselves what we want. I know it's not always as easy as it sounds. There are all kinds of injunctions, internal and cultural, that tell us either directly or subconsciously not to do this. A few examples of these messages are:

I don't deserve this.

It's inappropriate for me to do something like this.

They should just do it for me.

It's not nice, or right, to think of myself first.

Practicing Self-kindness may take time; it takes courage to step out of your comfort zone and learn how to give to yourself.

Understand this is not about adopting a self-centered, "me, me, me" way of behaving. Rather, it's an intentional way of being in which you take better care of yourself beyond how you usually take care of yourself. This helps you to be happier in life as your self-esteem rises.

We can see this idea clearly by inverting the well-known Golden Rule.

Do unto others as you would have them do unto you.

Into…

Do unto yourself as you would have others do unto you.

Or as some teachers say, *treat yourself how you desire others to treat you.*

> In this section you'll take it a step further with Question #2. *(How could the people you know, treat you more kindly?)*
>
> For each entry, pause and ask, *If they did what I'd like them to do for me, what could I do for them in return, as an act of kindness?* What you do in return isn't about it being something big, or even equal to what you want from them. This is about giving. You want to consider little things as well.
>
> Write down your answers.

Can you imagine doing kind things towards that person without them first doing something kind for you? Doing it simply because you want to be kind?

I had this experience at a very important period in my life.

My mother died when I was 22. One evening some months after her death, my father and I were sitting in his bedroom watching TV when a thought started rattling around in my head that I had never told him I loved him. I felt agitated thinking about this, even while knowing it wasn't entirely true. I knew for sure I'd told him a long time before when I was younger, and I really wanted to tell him right then. It wasn't a comfortable thing for me to do. When the next commercial came on I screwed up my courage and said in a weak, constrained voice, "Dad, you know, ummm…I love you."

"I love you too," he said. "What's on channel 2, no channel 4, maybe channel 5 …?"

I was mortified. I had bared my soul and he'd responded with light chatter about TV channels! I stewed with feeling how wrong that was for a while until I got that I didn't do it to hear how much he loved me, I'd told him for me. *I wanted him to know I loved him.*

Perhaps maybe I did want to hear it. Maybe hearing him say he loved me was the thing I wanted most from him. Yet, I had no control over my dad's response, my control stopped with what I did. I wanted my dad to know how I felt about him.

From then on, instead of waiting for him to say he loved me, I'd periodically tell him I loved him. It always felt awkward, because I wasn't used to saying it. I did it, and it felt good.

A few months later, talking on the phone with my father, an amazing thing happened. Just as we were getting off, I thought I heard him mumble, "I love you." I wasn't sure I heard right! The next time we spoke, he said it again. And he continued to say it from then on. We both did.

I changed my behavior towards my dad. It's true I wanted him to say he loved me, too; yet, the important part is I took care not to bring expectations to our interactions. I centered myself in my desire for him to know how I felt, and my desire to express kindness towards him. Over time, it resulted in a change in his behavior. One that touched me deeply.

Sometimes getting the things we want from others takes time. Rather than wait for someone else to act kindlier first, we can decide to take the first step. We can be genuinely kind, with or without ever getting what we want. Although it's not guaranteed, when we take an action in the direction of kindness, something will shift. Nearly always the shift is in ourselves, yet, perhaps not in the other person. It's almost magical how this happens, and it goes back to the previous discussions about our feelings, thoughts, and sensations being tied to each other. A shift in one causes a shift in the others.

Let's see how this may work for you. If, for example, you want your partner to make you coffee in the morning, and you make it yourself instead. Make it for both of you. *Be clear within yourself you're not doing this to get something back, or as a way of manipulating them into making coffee for you.* Do it as a way of being kind to yourself and to them. Give it time. You may find one day they're making you coffee. Perchance you'll find you like your new role as the coffee maker, and no longer want them to do it. A huge benefit is you being kinder to yourself and you being easier
on yourself.

If you live alone, think of something you can do for a friend that you'd like them to do for you. Perhaps you can treat them to a movie or make them a meal. Maybe you can offer to run an errand for them when you're already going out to do something for yourself.

> *"Self-acceptance is my refusal to be in an adversarial relationship to myself."*
> ~ Nathaniel Brand

One big way you can be a kinder to yourself is to be easier on yourself. Most people I know, including myself, are too hard on themselves, too judgmental, too unforgiving, too critical. We expect too much of ourselves and think we have to be the best, be right, be the smartest. One huge habitual pattern I see in adult learners is thinking they must be good at doing something immediately, before they've ever done it. I've mentioned this before. Remember the young man who wanted to be the best practitioner in Feldenkrais, communicating everything perfectly, before he even started? How realistic is that?

The other important point is to allow yourself time to develop a new ability, including allowing yourself the freedom to make mistakes and explore.

Hubert Dreyfus, a linguist from the University of California-Berkeley, describes in his article "The Current Relevance of Merleau-Ponty's Phenomenology of Embodiment" the five stages of learning --- novice, advanced beginner, competence, proficient and expertise. These stages directly relate to what I'm encouraging you to do.

"Competence," is a particularly interesting stage to me because Dreyfus offers a surprising definition that is not typically considered as "competence". His definition of "competence" is:

> "With more experience, the number of potentially relevant elements of a real-world situation the learner is able to recognize becomes overwhelming. At this point, since a sense of what is important in any particular situation is missing, performance becomes nerve-wracking and exhausting, and the student might wonder how anybody ever masters the skill."[3]

Performance that is overwhelming, nerve-wracking and exhausting leads to COMPETENCE!

Everyone who has ever set out to learn anything has experienced these feelings at one time or another along the way to feeling competent. Understanding this is part of the journey toward competence will help you stay the course and get to be "competent" in the things you do with kindness to yourself.

Everything goes back to self-perception; expect yourself to be good at your endeavor, sincerely try to like yourself, and value yourself as worthy of kindness.

Placing impossible standards on yourself is a no-win proposition; expecting to be good at something right away is an impossible standard. You may intellectually know it's silly, and still fall into the trap of unrealistic expectations. In the end, you create suffering for yourself with thoughts that don't serve your greatest and kindest good.

If you find yourself struggling with negative self-talk (meaning, how you talk to yourself) about how good you are, consider the above definition of competence. See if you can take your negative self-talk down a notch, from *"I'm not good enough,"* to *"I'm doing the best I can."*

(A full description of Dreyfus' all five stages of learning is in the appendices in the back of this book along with a link for the entire article.)

My Mantra that Works

If your compassion does not include yourself, it is incomplete.
~ Jack Kornfield

Several years ago I was feeling tired as I returned from a long working stint in Europe. Since I had a lot of additional work coming up, while on the plane I reviewed the things I had to get done upon arriving at home. I became completely overwhelmed with the material I was working on, much in the way Dreyfus describes the experience of the competent learner.

As the feeling of overwhelm overtook me, I caught myself. I noticed what was happening and questioned myself. Was this really a good time to be thinking about this material? With this awareness and my question, something shifted in me. I actually laughed out loud because the answer was completely obvious. Of course, it wasn't a good time. I had worked hard, non-stop for a month. I was spent, out of gas. I needed time to recuperate, and this plane trip was not the best place for making my To Do list.

Whenever I'm able to catch myself having negative thoughts or feeling overwhelmed, if I stop to ask if it's a good time to be thinking about whatever is going on, the answer is always an emphatic No.

I'm not using this as an excuse to avoid what has to be done. It's the recognition that this moment is not the best time to think about the tasks that lie ahead of me. Each time I do this it represents a moment when I'm a bit less critical of myself, a bit easier on myself and a bit kinder to myself.

Is this a good time to be thinking about this? has become my mantra, the thing I repeat whenever I feel inundated by the world. It works, because it frees me to take care of myself.

Importantly, the first thing is to be able to catch yourself, and it can't stop there. You must find something you can do about it, because if all you do is become aware of the feeling of overwhelm you'll tend to increase the overwhelm feelings. Awareness isn't enough, nor does it serve you by itself. Awareness is the first step. Finding a way to redirect your thoughts and feelings that allows you to breathe a bit easier is the next step. Our mantra addresses this step.

More About Mantras

Mantras are words repeated to aid concentration. I'm sharing two additional mantras from a therapist I worked with. These mantras helped me be kinder and easier with myself. For me, they're particularly useful in interrupting the darker places I can find myself in.

You know those times when negative thoughts loop incessantly around and around in your head, it's the circular rumination that goes nowhere. No questions answered. No new actions made. We all can fall under their spell now and then, and it's frustrating. What can you do about them?

Whenever I catch myself in one of these endless, negative conversations, I stop and say to myself, "I am driving around in a bad neighborhood. I need to get out of here." This helps me identify what's happening, and I say it as often as I need to, to help me move on. If the thoughts return and start their loop again (and they usually do), I once again remind myself it's time to get out of that bad neighborhood.

Over time, with practice, you will become effective at not getting caught by these kinds of thoughts. They may return. It's part of being human. Your task is getting effective in dealing with them in the same way you spend less time driving around in a bad neighborhood.

The last mantra is similar; however, it is quite specific. This mantra is useful when you're in a different, endless conversation in which you keep asking what if? The real problem with 'what if' conversations is they almost always involve something you can't know the answer to. Examples are: What if I lose my job? What if my partner leaves me? What if I win the lottery? You're left with speculations or making plans without adequate information.

No matter if it appears positive, it's a dead end. The next time you're driving around in a bad neighborhood in your head, maybe you'll find you're actually at a dead end! Perhaps, the mantra I am at a dead end will serve you. Then, you let it go, because you know this thought isn't going anywhere, there is no way I can answer this question.

I offer these mantras as a way to represent different ways of interrupting your habitual thought patterns. Using them will also give you the feeling of being easier with yourself and kinder to yourself. They can bring you a sense of relief and provide you with a sense of hope and freedom by releasing you from the negative thoughts and feelings that interfere with your liking yourself more. This is all about kindness.

The fifth step to creating and living in a kinder world... being kinder with yourself and others...

Treating yourself a little bit better and using mantras

Simple action steps:

1. From the list, identify something you want someone else to do for you, and do it for yourself. Do it with the intention of being kinder to yourself and you deserve it. Not because it's in reaction to not getting something,

2. From the list you generated in response to the question *How could the people you know treat you more kindly?* Select one person (more if you like) and identify ways you can act kindlier towards them, without them changing how they are toward you first.

3. Use your mantras — *Is this a good time to be thinking about this? I am driving around in a bad neighborhood; I need to get out of here. This is a dead end* — when you find yourself doing or thinking about something when it's not the right place or time, and when your thoughts are running in loops. Practice interrupting yourself with the mantra in the middle of the behavior until it becomes a habit. You decide which ones work best in which moments.

4. When you find you're having unkind thoughts about yourself, such as "I'm not good enough," "I'll never learn this," or "Everyone's better at this than I am," add onto each thought, *"And I'm doing the best I can."* It's unlikely you'll get rid of these thoughts right away; adding that last reassurance of 'you're okay' will give you a better chance at moving forward.

I am not good enough.

And... I am doing the best I can!

Is this a good time to be thinking about this?

No.

I'm driving around in a bad neighborhood.

I need to get out of here.

I'm at a dead end.

Time to move on.

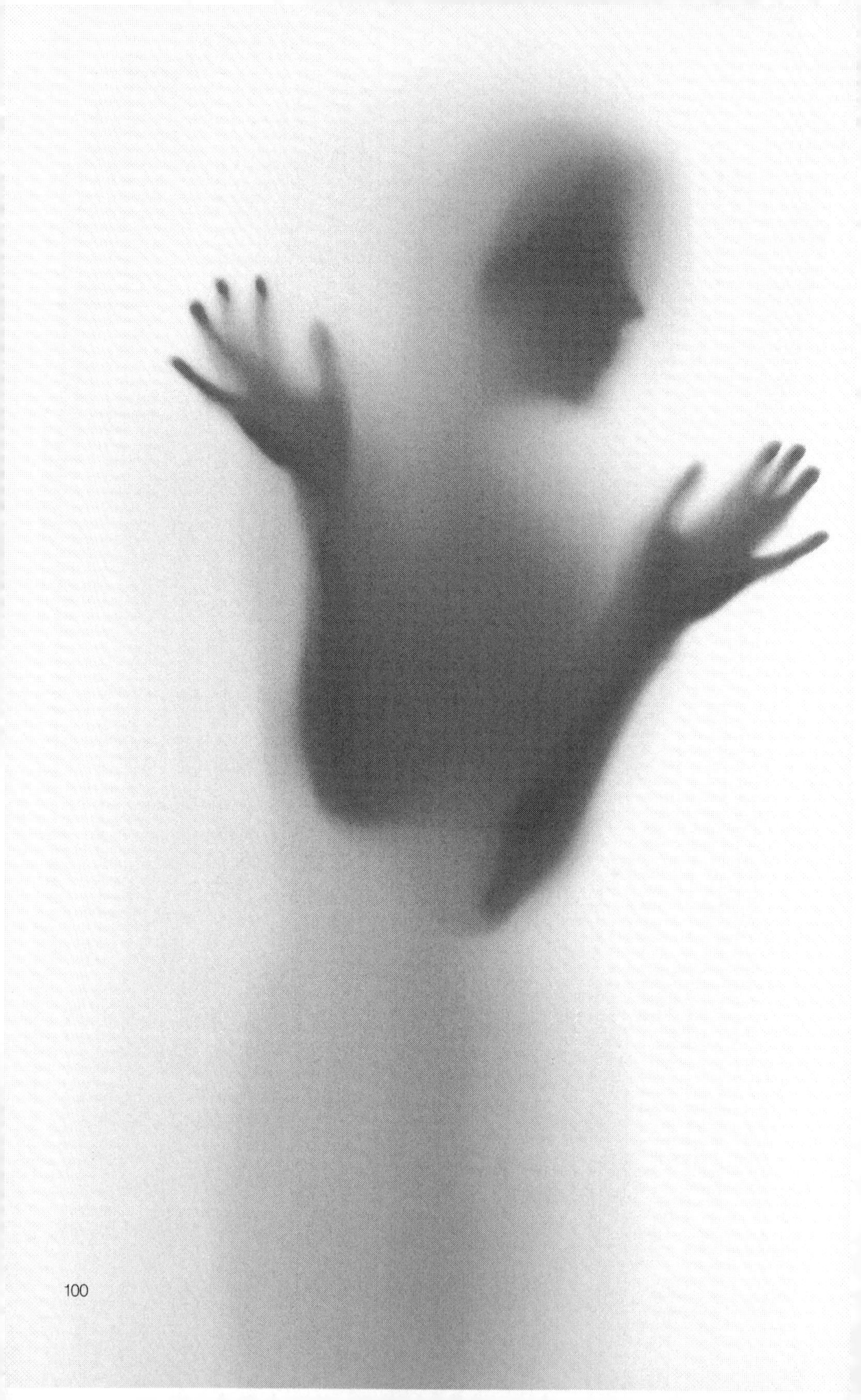

"Nothing is more revealing than movement." – Martha Graham

CHAPTER SIX

It's All in How You Move

In the previous chapter we looked at the concept of liking yourself and its positive impact on your capacity for kindness. We examined certain aspects that will help you learn to practice kindness to yourself.

Additionally, I illustrated that many of our ideas around how much you like yourself is attached to external outcomes, external expectations, and external definitions of success; these are the details of your everyday life, your job, your relationships.

We reviewed why your jobs and relationships aren't the best places for making change — at least, initially — because they're external measures; connected with outcomes, attachments and success. Plus, most work environments don't offer the safety, time, or support to pursue liking oneself more, particularly in any consistent way. You're at work to get the job done that you were hired to do.

Your relationships may appear to be great place to learn to like yourself more and you think relationships may help you discover the ways you don't like yourself. Yes, relationships can help; yet, the challenge is in the complexity that exists in relationships, including how the other person(s) feel about themselves and the dynamics set up between you. These factors can be counter-productive to your progress in exploring your feelings, thoughts, and sensations around your own self-esteem. Relationships can get in the way, because it's never entirely about you. It's always about the other person(s) and what's going on for them, as well.

The old saying "stop and smell the roses" comes into play at this moment in time: How busy are you? Where are the spaces in your life for this current exploration and new adjustment?

It's important to have an arena that feels safe, with space and time to listen and feel your Inner Self. You will need a place easy to access throughout your day; whether at work or play, whether alone or in a relationship. This place will be a part of your everyday life, and yet, distinct from it.

Are you groaning and thinking yeah, right. . .where would that be?. For now, hold the thought. I promise we'll get back to it shortly.

Pleasure

Complete this sentence: I feel pleasure when I . . .

You can consider this from whatever point of view guides you — a cultural point of view, your family values, your religious beliefs, your ideas around your age, the beliefs you hold, etc. Every person is guided in their own way. In your world, where does pleasure come in? When in your life do you give yourself permission to feel pleasure?

I ask this question often. Usually the answers are the same: playing sports, dancing, playing an instrument, having sex, eating, sleeping, exercising, taking walks, shopping, talking with friends or going to movies. A few people include working, their job.

Take your time — think — **What are your ways?**

How much time each day do you engage in pleasurable activities? My guess it falls short of five hours a day if you add it all up together.

Have you ever looked at a 24-hour day, and how you spend it? Subtracting 7-8 hours for sleep, **what do you do with the other 16 hours?** There's time for eating and bathing; if you have a job or school, there is time spent there. If you're lucky, work or school can count as pleasure time. Perhaps you watch TV or play video games, which can count as pleasure time. **What else do you do? And in these hours, how much time is spent on things that make you feel good?** In other words, feel a sense of pleasure.

Here is a question you may never have thought of answering...**do you think you could tolerate more pleasure?** By definition, 'to tolerate' something means to allow it without interfering. The answer to this question is vital to your experience of pleasure in your life; why is this? — because every single person has a threshold for the amount of pleasure they believe is appropriate or acceptable. When this threshold is crossed, anxiety and discomfort can set in and thoughts of *I don't deserve to feel this good* or *Something bad will follow* can show up.

This is not to suggest you need to feel pleasure all the time. If you do feel pleasure continuously you may not realize it; contrast of feelings helps you know what each feeling means and how it feels. Through this difference, distinctions are made.

Imagine all possible feelings are arranged on a continuum; from what's extremely pleasant to you on one end, to extremely unpleasant or painful on the other end. As you move back and forth along the continuum, you will have different experiences. Where you spend the most time on the continuum can make a big difference in your life.

For example, if you feel utterly miserable most of the time, simply feeling bad can feel like a vast improvement. What about feeling good? — rather than comparing feeling bad to feeling miserable, you can compare feeling bad to feeling good, or feeling good to feeling better… and feeling good to feeling great!

Experiencing a sense of pleasure can make you smile; when accompanied by a feeling of satisfaction, will, in turn, influence the attitudes you bring to the things you do. Without sufficient pleasure life can feel mundane and leave you wishing for a different life.

The bottom line is every single person needs a sufficient amount of pleasure in their life to like themselves; the amount needed is probably more than they have presently.

The all-important question: How do you increase your pleasure quotient? Where do you look?

Getting comfortable in your self

When do you get comfortable? Meaning, what are you doing when you feel comfortable?

Is this a silly question? Think on it. What if I said you'll discover you may be living your life in a rather odd way.

Among the answers I get when I ask "When do you get comfortable?' are: when I want to relax; when I go to bed; at the end of day; after I exercise; when I'm with my kids; when I'm with my grandchildren. The most frequent answer, one that seems true for everyone, is *we decide to get comfortable when we are uncomfortable.* Of course! This makes perfect sense.

And yet, if you consider the logic in that answer, it means you have to feel *uncomfortable before you decide to make yourself comfortable.* How did that happen?!

Let's consider the infant or young child as an example, again. What criteria does an infant, or a young child use to assess their sense of wellbeing? The answer is the same for every one of them: comfort. If they're hungry, they cry. When they're fed, they're content. If an infant's diaper is irritating them, or the child feels bad, they cry. Once what's bothering them is removed, they're happy again. Seems pretty simple and logical, right?

Children use comfort as their primary way of maintaining a sense of equilibrium and wellbeing. They actually seek out this feeling… or sensation… or both. This is the place where it becomes hard to distinguish between the feeling and the sensation, because it goes back and forth, and the boundaries are easily blurred.

In addition, a child needs to feel good to continue whatever they're doing. If they don't, they stop. Watch a child on the floor drawing with crayons: they move here and there, constantly changing position, they can remain engaged for a very long time. Seriously, can you imagine a child standing up after drawing on the floor for an extended time; and says, "Mommy, my hip hurts from sitting so long." I bet you can't. The reason is they've been monitoring themselves the whole time. Without knowing it, they've been paying attention, listening within themselves, for that state of wellbeing. When they feel the slightest sensations of discomfort, they change their position or what they're doing; they adapt until they have the feeling of wellbeing again. They continually change based on how they feel.

Yet, children don't always get to do things simply because it feels good to them. Growing up is a negotiation that involves continual learning and includes a multitude of elements. In school they learn to behave, stay at their desks, and sit still. They may be taught playing on the floor is unacceptable when wearing nicer clothes. All of the lessons taught relate to how they (rightly or wrongly) can fit in.

At the same time, learning these various elements of growing up teaches and conditions them to ignore certain aspects of themselves. Eventually they learn to override their feelings and sensations in favor of what they are 'supposed' to do. All of these lessons are to prepare them to become proper adults.

Does this sound familiar in any way? Do you ignore your feelings and sensations to do what must get done, or do what is expected of you? Let's look at how it fully manifests in us as adults.

As adults, most of us have learned to ignore ourselves to such a degree we're often uncomfortable, occasionally extremely uncomfortable. We may feel discomfort to the point of feeling stiff or in pain before we adjust our bodies to make ourselves comfortable. We've learned to place our attention on the external world; we have forgotten to simply listen to our bodies and listen to our feelings. We've learned to be unkind to ourselves.

It is essential to balance your ability to be and act in the world with how you feel inside; to re-establish this connection within you, to value it as you spontaneously did when you were younger. Just as you learned early on to ignore how you feel, you can learn to reverse the process. You can learn to seek — and find — more comfort and pleasure throughout your day.

Remember the discussion earlier about self-image being comprised of different components? Movement, how you physically act in the world, is of great importance here.

Movement

Movement has several important qualities. Tuning into these different qualities and noticing them can help you generate a deeper level of self-understanding. Developing a greater awareness of how you tend to move also gives you insight into how you tend to do things in general. This creates opportunities for new learning, which in turn can help you like yourself more.

Specifically, the first qualities to attend to are the size and speed of your movements. If you can learn to move slower and reduce the size of your movements, you can more easily bring your attention to what you're doing and how you're doing it.

A particularly important quality is the feeling a movement generates in you. You want to move in a way in which you *like how it feels.*

Is this a strange idea to you? — it's not unusual to think this way. We are not used to attending to our own comfort with this attention to detail or awareness of our movement.

Lowering the Threshold

Learning to lower your threshold of discomfort begins when you start developing a natural way of moving that feels good most of the time. You want to notice your own discomfort the minute it starts; there are many signals that precede the moment you actually feel uncomfortable. Discovering how to tune into these signals is the first step.

You can take this farther. When you're already feeling comfortable, discover how you can get more comfortable. You don't have to wait to be uncomfortable to do it! Pleasure and pain exist constantly on a back-and-forth continuum, as do comfort and discomfort. You can always move on that continuum; there is always an opportunity to go a little further to find greater comfort.

Another important aspect is: this allowing yourself to feel discomfort — then, taking actions in response to create more comfort — this ability to take action is self-caring and compassionate. Too often being self-compassionate and setting health goals, particularly with respect to exercise, aren't considered one and the same. Although not a scientific study, the essay by Psychologists M.L. Terry and M.R. Leary, "Self-compassion, self-regulation, and health" illustrates how self-compassion affects your attitudes toward your body, and in response, how you treat it:

> "Although increased muscle strength promotes health, many people injure themselves by having a lower-level goal that involves lifting more weight than they can manage safely. A self- compassionate approach would promote comfort and satisfaction with realistic lower order goals, because self-compassionate people will recognize they can improve over time, and thus not feel pressured to engage in extreme or dangerous health goals."[1]

According to research on self-compassion in additional articles in the same journal, "Self and Identity", people who struggle with self-compassion have a tendency to set more unrealistic health goals. If they injure themselves as a consequence, they also judge themselves in a harsh way for not reaching those goals. This self-judgment promotes negative feelings instead of a sense of self-love.

In contrast, people with high self-compassion (self-kindness) will probably take better care of themselves, in general. They tend to set exercise goals that are both realistic and safe in the first place. They will more easily notice when something isn't good for them and take steps to change it before injuring themselves. In short, self-compassion has a place in our movements, and in the gym.

You may think I'm suggesting we only seek pleasure or comfort. Not so.

I grew up in the 1960s when the "free love" movement was in its ascendance. Part of what underlay that movement was the idea everything should always feel good, and if it didn't, we shouldn't do it. It was a nice idea, yet impractical. Because as attractive as that thought may sound, life is more complicated, and we can't always do things based solely on what feels good. Often things need to get done regardless of how we feel; as a result, there is frequently an expense to our bodies, self-esteem, and satisfaction in life.

How far are you willing to push before you stop to take care of yourself? The correct answer is: not to the point where it's injurious. You can tolerate certain degrees of discomfort for a period of time. Simply be aware you're doing it and put the brakes on before things go too far.

To summarize, below are two new important insights into your general state of being:

1. Experiencing more pleasure and comfort are key to learning to like yourself more. If you are more comfortable in the everyday things you do, you can create additional pleasure in your life.

2. The greater the pleasure and comfort you find throughout your day, the more you will like yourself. If you like yourself more, you are likely to appreciate others to a greater degree, from there, more and more kindness will emerge.

Are you ready, perhaps eager, to make a change for greater pleasure and comfort in your life?

In actuality, this is not the best approach for a number of reasons. For one, doing more in a busy or full life is usually not sustainable or realistic. You can find time to go on longer walks or dance more, — the question is; do you know how to do it so you don't compromise or trade something else important? The answer doesn't lie in doing more.

Once again, it's important you approach this new understanding gently and with kindness towards yourself.

Look at the important pieces of how to do this in your life.

Is there a good place to practice doing something you like doing that feels good? A place where you feel safe and have the time to tune into your thoughts, feelings, and sensations? A place that you can access throughout your day, whether you're at work or play, alone or in relationship. A place that's part of, yet distinct from the essential things in your everyday life that doesn't require a great deal of effort?

I'm here to tell you there is, and it's going to sound radically simple.

All that is important is this one moment in movement. Make the moment important, vital, and worth living. Do not let it slip away unnoticed and unused.
～ Martha Graham

I'm going to propose a safe arena where you can begin to practice finding more pleasure and seeking more comfort in your everyday life. This practice is not powerfully or overtly connected to your job, school, relationships, or any other thing you're involved with. It's one where you can practice daily, almost without anyone knowing you're doing it.

As I explained in Chapter Two, and spoke about earlier in this chapter, the fourth aspect of your self-image is your movement or actions. This, along with your sensations, will be one of the main pathways for learning to like yourself more, and being kinder to yourself.

What's great about movement is how immediately accessible and solidly grounded it is. Movement is in everything you do! Additionally, you know immediately when you change how you move. While it is part of everything you do, it's rarely your focus. You simply move and do things. You focus on the task and not each movement how you do it.

Movement is also directly related to your sensations. You probably know the feeling of moving well, and the pleasure it can bring you. If you think about it, you can probably know how much better you feel about yourself when you move well, too.

It is through movement that you can make yourself more comfortable. This is the better place where you feel safe and comfortable, a place you practice experiencing more pleasure and creating more comfort for yourself. Plus, you can utilize movement as a source of liking yourself more.

The good news... it's easy, because it is using your attention and being guided by how much you like how it feels. It's not about working hard, or exercising, or being strong, or flexible. This is not about working harder. Working harder will set you up for failure, or seem impossible to achieve consistently.

Maybe you don't think of yourself as a 'movement' person. If that's the case, good news; it doesn't matter. This goal is feeling good while moving, not being good at moving. It can be as simple as walking from your desk to the water cooler or the sofa to the kitchen; it is a chance to check in with your body, how you feel in the moment and take pleasure in moving. You can do it any time; washing the dishes, making the bed, getting in and out of your car or taking a walk. In short, you can do it any moment at any time of day.

The reason it works is in all the little moments you create greater comfort and pleasure will add up to bigger moments. These bigger moments will shift how you relate to and respond to yourself and others.

You're learning to have a relationship with yourself focused on treating yourself kindlier; every moment you do this provides you with a different foundation of who you are and how you feel about yourself. It's from this foundation that you act with more kindness.

How you move in the world can give you more kindness in your life..

Consciousness is only possible through change, change is only possible through movement.

~ Aldous Huxley

The sixth step to creating and living in a kinder world... being kinder with yourself and others...

Getting comfortable and moving in ways that 'you like the way' it feels

Now it's time to explore how you find pleasure in simply moving.

Get out your notebook

Write down the places in your life where you experience pleasure. Include the small moments, like the first sip of a good cup of coffee or the momentary glance at a beautiful sunset, along with the big moments.

Consider what gives you pleasure on a particular day of the week, and list those.

When you've completed your list — sit with it for a few minutes; then, as you read each entry reflect on how you feel in each of those moments.

See if you can specifically identify the sensations you have in each instance, and where you feel them in your body.

Are they in your face... your chest... several places at once?

Think about how you move when you feel them.

Do these sensations differ with different experiences?

Notice how the expression on your face feels. Often our faces subconsciously reveal how we're feeling.

These sensations will be part of what you look for in the next exercises. You have a choice to do either 1, 2 or 3, or all of them. Do whichever works best for you.

1. **Look for moments in your day where you can explore the quality of how you feel when you move.** Pick simple tasks. Ones you do frequently throughout the day are great; getting in and out of bed, cleaning the house, or getting dressed are a few examples.

    While doing each task, slow your movements down just a little and find a way to move that you like the way it feels.

    Feel each part of your body and notice if you smiling or thinking it feels good? That will tell you when you're there. Let yourself feel good doing it.

    Interchange the tasks you focus on throughout your week or month if that makes it more interesting or fun.

2. Set an alarm to go off every hour, or every two or three hours... you decide. This can be on your phone; use what is convenient. When your alarm goes off, continue what you're doing and change it around to a focus on moving in a way that you like the way it feels. For example, sitting at the computer where you don't move much, take the moment to get a little more comfortable

in your chair, or perhaps adjust the screen and place your feet in a different position. If you aren't able to do this when the alarm goes off, let it go and wait for the next alarm.

3. Throughout the day, pause and consider if you feel comfortable.

If you do, make a small adjustment to get more comfortable, move to where you feel good. If you don't feel comfortable, see what small adjustment you can do so you are. Do this throughout your entire day whenever you think about it.

Continue expanding on it from this moment on until it feels as though it is second nature, and you don't need to remind yourself because it happens spontaneously.

PART THREE
Cultivating Kindness Towards Others

Spread love everywhere you go:
First of all,
in your own house...
kindness in your face
kindness in your eyes,
kindness in your smile,
kindness."

~ **Mother Teresa**

CHAPTER SEVEN

Kindness... 5 minutes a day...

The impetus to write this book came from my personal experiences with kindness and my inquiry into it for myself. As I shared in the story about my father in the introduction, I have him to thank for much of this.

I'd always considered myself kind, in a general way. I never thought it was something I needed to develop further until my father lost all his money and needed my help. I was reluctant, perhaps a bit resentful, yet, I gave him money anyway. I made the commitment. I had to override my initial thoughts and feelings to fulfill my commitment.

Over time I discovered my willingness to support him was a great gift. I saw it as a reflection of an innate kindness inside me and in my brother I didn't know was there. I was being kinder than I imagined; it helped me feel good about myself, and I liked myself more.

I also learned there are times we must act in the direction of creating more kindness, despite how we initially feel. Importantly, when it comes to kindness, it's action that matters. We can't wait for our thoughts and feelings to lead the way. Acting in line with our values (kindness being at the top of my list) leads to our thoughts and our feelings catching up and transforming.

Notably, I learned kindness is an innate, inner capacity that can be developed and cultivated. What is vital in cultivating kindness is taking action. Again, acting with the intention of being kind is the key to positive change.

My journey of discovery into kindness became even especially significant when my father aged and developed dementia. My stepmother, who attended to his care, reached a point she was unable to do it any longer; and after long discussions, we arrived at the decision to place him into a long-term assisted care facility.

My father was wintering in Florida at the time; which worked well, considering the climate, the availability and the cost of assisted care facilities. We found a place that was nice — at least nicer than most places where the inhabitants are struggling with connection to this world. The location was close to their winter home and my stepmother could regularly visit.

Then June came, and she went back to her apartment in New York, where her children and grandchildren lived. I realized my father was alone with no one to visit him; I grew concerned of the effect of loneliness on him.

This was the moment I acted, not understanding what I was doing or getting myself into. I made the decision to call him every day. For me, this was huge. Many adults speak with their parents every day. I rarely spoke with my dad twice in one month. This decision was significant.

We lived in different times zones; and although I thought the three-hour time difference was going to be a problem, it worked out well. He was predictably in his room at the time I was able to call. Our calls were typically about 5 minutes. Frequently the conversation was practically non-existent. Often there was no conversation. Sometimes he put the phone down and walked around while talking. On those calls, I was unable to hear him, and of course, he didn't hear me yelling he needed to return to the phone. At other times, he had the wrong end of the phone to his ear; while I was able hear him, he was unable to hear me. Unsurprisingly, the struggles and problems increased as his condition deteriorated.

I was fortunate he always knew who I was. His conversations may not have made sense, yet, he knew it was me he talked to everyday.

It wasn't long before calling every day became a habit; which wasn't easy, because I didn't *feel* like doing it. When I thought about calling, I felt irritated, sad, or bothered. I did it anyway, Eventually, over time, I moved beyond the hard feelings and the calls morphed into one more thing I did on a daily basis, like brushing my teeth.

This entire experience helped me think about what had changed. I never felt irritated, sad, or bothered when I brushed my teeth, and it was a necessary obligation, also. Albeit, it was not the same as one's relationship with one's father who has dementia. Nevertheless, in both instances, the regular act of doing what I did brought about a change in me.

Our feelings and thoughts and sensations can shift and change over time. We can be angry with someone. In the heat of the moment, the feeling is intense; we can't imagine it being any different. After a while or as time passes, we discover it's hard to stay angry; the initial intensity of anger can diminish and is difficult to sustain.

The same thing happened with calling my father. I'd lost the intensity of my initial feelings of being bothered, irritated and sad. To my surprise, I developed new feelings I never expected that replaced my original feelings.

My feelings of irritation changed to acceptance. My feelings of being bothered became a feeling of humor. (Honestly, life is just funny sometimes.) My feelings of sadness moved between occasionally feeling a bit low to a softer, gentle melancholy.

I called my dad every day for nearly three years. This was the closest I ever got to him. As time went on, his talk turned to mostly gibberish. Yet, he always appeared to know what I was talking about. These calls forged a bond between us that had never been there before; the effect lingered for months after he passed on. I still woke up each morning, reached for the phone to call, then, remembered he was no longer alive.

Previously I noted kindness is a skill, and a skill requires practice. The act of calling my father was the way I learned this. My daily calls to him presented challenges on multiple levels. The outcome (how I felt), the way I viewed staying connected, and the change in my relationship with my father made it all worthwhile. It was deeply rewarding. I learned more from that 5-minute act of calling my father every day than I had from any other act of kindness I've done before or since. Unbeknownst to me, I was practicing something that has served me until this day.

As a result of that practice, calling my father, I developed a practice of calling a number of people in my life regularly as an act of kindness. Some are old and some not very old. Many of them tell me how good it makes them feel when I call. Others don't say a thing about it, and I still know they're happy I call. Sometimes we talk for only a minute or two, other times for half an hour or more.

I learned to do something else through this practice, *I call regularly regardless of how I feel in the moments before I call.* I switch perspective if I feel I don't want to talk to someone; I think instead on their pleasure of getting a call from me. Then, I simply call the person.

I always feel better afterwards. My outlook on the rest of my day changes. I have different thoughts than I previously had, and I experience those thoughts in a different way. How you act can be differentiated from your feelings, and those feelings can change in relation to our actions.

Five minutes a day spent with my father changed my thoughts and feelings in ways I never imagined. Maybe five minutes a day spent in an act of kindness can change your life, too.

Where is Your Five minutes a day?

Think, again, about all the things you do in a day and how you spend your time. How many hours in one day do you spend at work, or cooking, or eating, or watching TV, or browsing the internet or texting/talking on your phone? Our days are filled with numerous activities we don't measure. Our nature is to repeatedly engage in our normal, everyday life without thinking about it.

Time may be standardized, yet, it's interesting to consider how exceedingly elastic time can feel. You know the feeling. Time can fly, or slow down, or appear to stop; depending on what you're doing, where you are, or who you're with.

I'll go back to the example of brushing my teeth. Dentists advise we brush for two minutes, twice a day. In clock time, that's not long at all; and yet, have you had the experience when it felt like a long time? There are electric toothbrushes with timers built in to remind you to shift to another quadrant of your mouth every thirty seconds. If you'd been brushing manually and switch over to an electric toothbrush, you may think the timer isn't working properly, that it can't be possibly be correct, because thirty seconds feels so long. Other times, you think you missed the beep when it really isn't time for it. Time is relative, plain and simple. It is relative to the task, to our thoughts and desires, to our feelings and emotions, and to the sensations we feel in our bodies.

Let's explore how five minutes, which doesn't appear to be a long time, may feel. This can be an interesting experiment.

There are 12 *five-minute periods* in an hour.

...60 *five-minute periods* between 7AM and noon...

...another 72 *five-minute periods* between noon and 6PM...

...and an additional 60 five-minute periods from 6PM till 11PM.

In total, 192 five-minute periods in one waking day between 7AM and 11PM.

Depending on the hours you keep, there may be additional five-minute periods in your day.

Look at your day. You may find it filled with five-minute tasks.

Write down all the tasks that involve another person: people at work, if you have children, include them, include your relationships, and include people you encounter when you're out and about. If you have a cat or dog, include the time you spend petting and grooming them.

Pause for a moment and reflect on your list. Are these things you see as five minutes really five minutes? Put a check next to those you truthfully see as five minutes.

Maybe some of your daily tasks require a great deal of your attention and time, while other tasks only a little bit of attention and time. I know when my dog was old, I decided to give him five minutes of my undivided attention every day, and it was hard to do.

The seventh step to creating and living in a kinder world... being kinder with yourself and others...

Five minutes a day

Now let's explore this concept of devoting FIVE minutes a day to an act of kindness. This is the most important process in the book; over time it can and will significantly shift your relationship with kindness. Please take the time needed to consider and practice this exercise; if now is not the right time to dive in, find time to come back and do it later.

You want to always appreciate what you can do and acknowledge your readiness when it's the right time.

If you fall down in the process and don't do what you intend, pick yourself up and begin again. It's that simple.

This exercise is about taking action. As you learned, your feelings may feel incongruent as you perform the task you chose to do each day; there may be a difference in how you feel before you do the task and the moment you do the task. Do it, and take action, anyway.

It will be easier to work with a person on your list with whom you're already acting kindly toward. It's also fine if you choose to work with another person on your list.

Spend five minutes a day directing your attention toward this person.

You can approach this in various ways. You can spend five minutes a day thinking about this person, wondering how they are or what they may be doing. Better yet, spend five minutes doing something you consider kind with or for them; talk with them on the phone, write them an e-mail, or sit quietly with them.

Do your five minutes all at one time, if possible. If not, do a few moments at a time throughout the day. Just do it, five minutes every day!

I recommend reminding yourself of your intention first thing in the morning when you wake; and again, before you sleep at night, take a few moments to reflect on your intention. I advise this because your life can get busy and remembering to do this is harder than you may imagine. It will help immeasurably to put a reminder note near your bed, on the refrigerator, or at your desk. If you discover you completely forgot, be kind with yourself. There's always the next day.

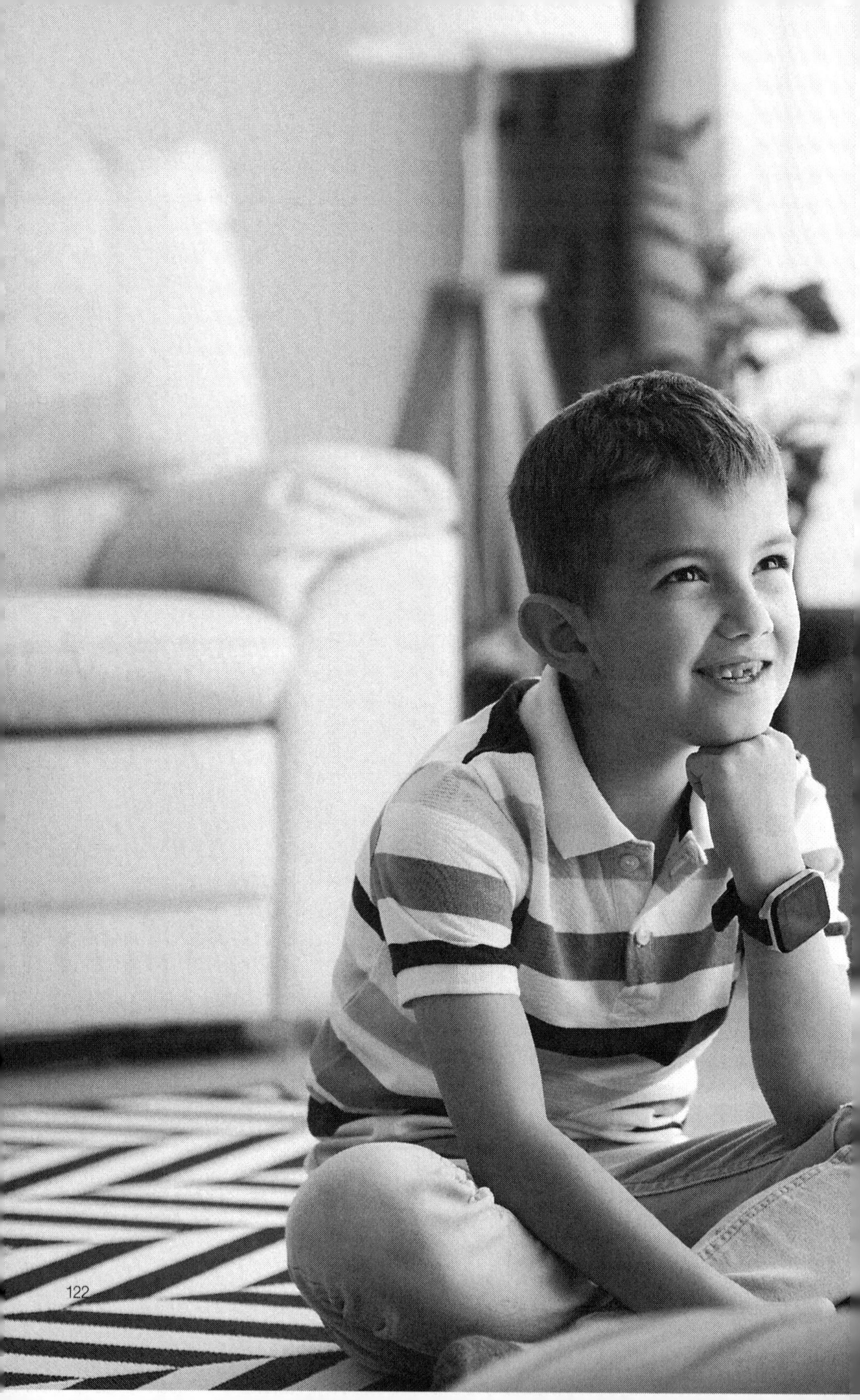

*Listening is a positive act:
 you have to put yourself out to do it*
   ~ **David Hockney**

CHAPTER EIGHT

Look... and Listen

There are multiple ways to show kindness to others. There are things you can do with them, and things you can do for them. Little things, big things, things every once in a while, and things you do daily. There are things you can do without being asked, and include doing things when you're asked.

Earlier, in your exploration with kindness, you made a list of people noting the ways in which you already demonstrate kindness, and you made a list of the ways you desire to demonstrate more kindness. This is a valuable beginning. The lists are just the tip of the iceberg. You may realize by now there are many more people in a day than you included on your lists. You may have been surprised at the myriad ways you can create acts of kindness each day. Ways that are easy, and yet, add up to big differences for you and the people you encounter and/or interact with each day.

Take a moment now, before you go on... think if in the past day, in the past week or in the past month there was an interaction that stood out for you because you felt someone showed a bit of kindness toward you. Did anyone do or say something that made you pause or smile? Did anyone make you feel a little bit better about yourself? Did that kindness come from someone you know, or from a stranger?

When another person acts kindly toward us, we are transported to a new feeling, and often this is a happier or more peaceful place. An act of kindness can bring a smile to our face, and this can work the other way around. You can create an equally special moment for another person and help make their day a bit better.

Small moments of kindness add up. They make a real difference for you, for others, and for the world we live in.

In the article "Mistakenly Seeking Solitude", researchers Nicolas Epley and Juliana Schroeder state:

"... commuters on a train into downtown Chicago reported a significantly more positive commute when they connected with a stranger than when they sat in solitude...People riding on a public bus had a more positive experience when they talked to a nearby stranger than when they sat in isolation..."[1]

What is possible, if, in addition to experiencing a few large acts of kindness every once in a while, you experienced numerous small acts of kindness scattered throughout your day? Can you imagine how you may feel at the end of the day? Can you imagine how you may feel when you wake up the next day?

Let's begin with something that almost everyone can appreciate when beginning to consider the many ways they can be kinder to others.

Again, I have never met anyone who doesn't want to like themselves more. This is an element I believe we all have in common. And I believe there is another element everyone wants, which is; they want to be seen, they want to be heard and they want to be listened to. What this means to/for each person may be different and may show up differently, yet, it's a universal desire. Scientific research validates this.

In the article "The Need to Belong: Desire for Interpersonal Attachments as Fundamental Human Motivation" authors Baumeister and Leary propose people need frequent personal contacts or interactions:

> "The desire for interpersonal attachments — the need to belong — is a fundamental human motivation," they write. And "The desire for interpersonal attachment may well be one of the most far-reaching and integrative constructs currently available to understand human nature."[2]

We create human connection when we're truly present with one another, and really listen to each other. Too often we're distracted or have our minds on another matter and forget to do this.

In the article, "Relationship Satisfaction among South Asian Canadians", researchers Saunia Ahmad & David W. Reid reference the work of F. K. Doell & D. W. Reid,

"Partners' listening styles and relationship satisfaction: The role of listening to understand vs. listening to respond". They have distinguished two variations in listening, both useful to understand. The two ways are listening to understand (LTU) and listening to respond (LTR)."[3]

"Listening to understand is characterized as a more proactive and intentional form of listening requiring more focused attention and sensitivity on the part of the listener to the verbal and nonverbal message of their partner. It indicates an underlying motivation to get at the deeper meaning or 'understanding' of what one's partner is trying to say…In contrast, listening to respond is commonplace and is characterized as a more automatic form of listening, a kind of jumping to conclusions that reflects listening only enough to react with their own response."[3]

This means listening to understand (LTU) is one of the kindest things you can do. It offers the other person a sense of belonging and connectedness. Being listened to deeply and attentively is important to our wellbeing, and a great deal of what people want and need, its importance is many times unknown and/or overlooked except in extreme circumstances. For these reasons, listening to understand
as a way of interacting may not be part of your daily routines.

It is a worthy intention. And when it comes to connecting with another being, the first step is simply to see them and acknowledge their presence, which can be the hardest step.

In my Feldenkrais practice, I've practiced listening to understand (LTU) tens of thousands of times. At first, I learned how to listen primarily through my hands and touch. Then, as I listened more deeply through my hands, my listening extended to my ears until, again and again, I was fully present with people without needing to speak aloud.

Fortunately, I've had a number of great teachers to remind me how important it is to relate by listening fully. Probably the best teacher was my dog, Sky, a border collie.

Sky looked for and found me throughout the day, asking for my attention, either he wanted to play or he wanted a treat. Typically, petting him for a few moments was sufficient; then, he went back outside and monitored everything around him (border collies tend to do this naturally).

His visits for attention felt like a moment of mutual acknowledgement to me. Yes, he wanted something from me, and he was giving me something, as well; acknowledgment I was there (being seen), and we had a relationship. Although it usually lasted only a few moments, it was long enough for a real exchange. Our exchange always demonstrated a moment of appreciation, sometimes him to me, sometimes me to him, and most often, mutual appreciation.

You may or may not have a pet, and I'm not suggesting it's the only way to have this kind of experience. I'm offering it as an example for this way interacting, where there's mutual exchange no matter who's doing the asking.

How's your day going?

Every time you smile at someone, it is an action of love, a gift to person, a beautiful thing.
~ Mother Teresa

Researchers Epley and Schroeder say:
> "Aristotle famously argued man is by nature a social animal, but people in the company of strangers often look to be anything but social. Instead of treating each other as possible sources of well-being, strangers in close proximity often ignore each other completely, treating each other more like objects than like fellow social beings. For one of the most highly social species on the planet, whose members benefit significantly from forming connections with other people, this seems paradoxical. Why would highly social animals in the company of strangers so routinely ignore each other?... Humans may indeed be social animals but may not always be social enough for their own well-being…This research broadly suggests people could improve their own momentary well-being—and of others—by simply being more social with strangers, trying to create connections where one

might otherwise choose isolation."[1]

Maybe you recognize yourself in the above description. How do you create connections? Or do you prefer to choose isolation? These possible ways of interacting with strangers gives new meaning to random chit chat and how we might or might not be present with another person. That moment you give another person your full attention can be one of the kinder things you can do.

New York City, where I grew up, has an unfair reputation of being unfriendly. New York is a friendly place; it's not noticed as the friendliness displayed there is manifested in different ways than other places. For one, New York is not a city where people greet others they don't know on the street with a "Hi." People tend to keep to themselves amid all the hustle and bustle. Yet they do help each other out; helping someone carrying packages, holding a door open for you, holding the bus while you are running to catch it.

Here's an example of atypical New Yorker behavior. Years ago, when a good friend, who I met in college, and I were both living in New York; he acted in a manner that was atypical of a born and bred New Yorker. His behavior struck me as odd, unusual and got my attention. This incident may not be unusual if you don't live in New York; crucial to this story is where it happened and what my friend did... what we call 'context.'

My friend and I went into the same New York City bank and stood in line, my friend directly in front of me. When he got to the teller, he gave her his deposit slip, within a minute into the transaction, he said, 'So how is your day going?' I saw the question stopped her cold. She looked at him for a moment before she smiled and said, 'Pretty good, how's yours going?'

Witnessing this stopped me cold, too. It made such an impression I still remember how I felt. I never considered asking a bank teller how they were doing. Yet, as I soon learned, this was normal behavior my friend displayed regularly. I don't know how he learned it; although I was puzzled, the incident opened my eyes. Through this interaction I began to see I encountered dozens of people each day without having a single moment of real connection.

If you are a Southerner this would be considered 'normal' behavior, but my friend was from the Bronx! I have no idea how he developed such a 'friendly' habit.

I wanted to change that. I wanted to create authentic connection and feel tangible connection throughout my day, every day.

Intentional chit chat

Love and kindness are never wasted. They always make a difference.
~ Barbara DeAngelis

I wish to make a distinction that what I'm talking about is not the nonspecific polite, "How are you?" … "Fine, thanks," or the "Have a nice day," kind of exchange that's become so common. I'm referring to a moment of acknowledgment, where a person feels seen and heard. A moment that draws them back into the present moment. What I wanted was moments where I consciously engaged with others. What I call *intentional chit chat*, where there's listening to truly understand that connection.

Intentional chit chat means you focus on the other person, even if it's only momentarily. You genuinely express an interest in them. It's not asking to find out their whole life story. It's enough to ask them a question and listen to their response with your full presence.

I began to intentionally practice engaging with someone for just long enough to let them know I knew they were there; to let them know they were more than another cog in the wheel of the machine of my day.

I really had to practice this, because it was not part of my nature to do it. Perhaps it is more accurate to say it was in my nature, a part I had never developed. Either way, it took practice to go outside of myself and interact with a stranger again and again.

At first it felt quite awkward, and then, over time it became fun and interesting. Seeing someone smile made me feel better, too!

Now, to those of us who are introverts, the idea of actively going out of our comfort zone to engage with another person may provoke nightmares. I understand. This is not a plan to over-ride your nature. The intention is to explore what is at the heart of your true nature and understanding how you know if your behavior in any moment is an expression of your nature or merely the product of certain habits you've been perpetuating.

We will take a closer look at our tendency to resist engaging with others; then, we'll explore how we can practice a way of being with others that feels okay, and even good.

Does pulling away help?

> *I don't like that man. I must get to know him better.*
> ~ Abraham Lincoln

Let's start by looking at an extreme example of engaging with someone you want to avoid.

I imagine you know or have met someone who demands your attention in a way that if you see them walking toward you, you immediately cross to the other side of the street. You believe with this one person there's no end to an interaction or no way out of a conversation if they hook you in. When you're with them it feels as if they want or need something from you, and that need is insatiable.

When you're in a conversation with this needy or overbearing person, you probably spend all your time looking for a way out, rather than listening to what they say. It's understandable that one could feel this way. Now, let's turn it around.

Can you imagine how this person might feel when you listen to them in this detached, get me out of here way? Can you place yourself in their shoes? Imagine how you would feel if when you're speaking with a person, the thing you feel most is that person wanting to get away.

Sadly, their experience probably doesn't only happen with you, most people may respond to them by pulling away. Imagine the effect this has on their personal self-worth, perhaps they don't know they do this or how to change their behavior patterns.

I had my own realization of this dynamic while on a plane, returning home from teaching in Switzerland. I had an aisle seat, and across the aisle from me were two women who were obviously strangers to each other. The middle-aged woman by the window was talking nonstop with a running commentary on everything she was seeing and feeling. Looking out the window, she commented on seeing her bag being loaded, simultaneously saying this was her first flight. Her inability to stop talking went beyond the normal excitement a person expresses on their first time flying.

Meanwhile, the Asian woman seated next to her was reading a book, doing her best to ignore her seatmate. The excited woman kept talking and asked the Asian woman if she was Japanese. Without giving the Asian woman time to reply, she exclaimed "I never met a Japanese person before." The Asian woman replied she was Korean. The excited woman said, "I never met anyone Korean, either." She continued her one-way conversation, nonstop.

I thought *whew, I sure am glad I'm not on an eight-hour flight sitting next to her.*

Sometime later, I glanced over and saw the Korean woman was gone, and the chatty woman was sitting alone. She lit up at the chance to make contact with me. I avoided her gaze. Sometime later still, I glanced over again to see the Korean woman back in her seat, and the other woman was now gone.

I couldn't resist, I asked the Korean woman what was going on. She said the other woman had been bothering her so much, she complained to the flight attendants who responded by giving her a seat in business class. When her seatmate heard this, she demanded to sit in business class, too! Therefore, the Korean woman returned to coach, and the chatty one was in business. I admit I felt sorry for whoever sat next to her in business class.

I must have napped for a while, the next time I glanced over, the Korean woman was gone and the chatty one was back. This time she succeeded in catching my eye. I immediately felt trapped and could feel myself pulling away in retreat from any engagement.

Then I caught myself and stopped. Instead of withdrawing, I actively engaged this woman in a conversation, giving her my full attention. We talked for a few minutes before I said, "I'm going to go back to reading my book now."

She smiled, nodded in agreement and left me alone after our brief conversation.

When I reflected on what I'd done and what happened, I was surprised. I'd had many interactions with people who felt this needy, yet, this was the first time I didn't pull away. What surprised me about the interaction most, though, was the relative ease I experienced in talking with her. In retrospect, my ability to really listen to her, made it easy to stop the conversation when I wanted to.

This woman probably too often has conversations in which the other person wants to pull away, leaving her feeling extremely unheard, diminished. In turn, these conversations may confirm (and therefore excite) her neediness.

"When you go out into the woods, and you look at trees, you see all these different trees. And some of them are bent… you sort of understand that it didn't get enough light, and so it turned that way. And you don't get all emotional about it. You just allow it. The minute you get near humans, you lose all that. And you are constantly saying 'You are too this, or I'm too this.' That judgment mind comes in. And so I practice turning people into trees. Which means appreciating them just the way they are."

~ Ram Dass

If this was my experience in a conversation, if I sensed the person I was talking to was pulling away, I'd probably want to hold onto them even more, too. This can be a terrible predicament to be in for both parties. One is desperately wanting attention, while the other desperately tries to figure out how not to get caught.

My example with the two women on the plane is extreme; the context we were in was clearly defined within a confined area with minimal options for contact with other people, and in a situation where there was little likelihood for future interactions. Considering the dynamics, we weren't likely going to become friends, either. Importantly, I learned I was able to engage without being swept away, as long as I fully engaged with the person. This awareness was a valuable take-away.

I've found myself in similar situations since then, and each time, while it takes my full intention, I've been able to engage and easily dis-engage.

I confess at times I worried a future encounter with another person (like the chatty woman) may lead to an undesired result. I'd think Uh oh, now they are going to think we are friends. I feared, by implication of previous exchanges where I paid attention and listened, I may be committing to an increase in number and length of my interactions with needy people. What I discovered is this hasn't been the case. As long as I'm clear I am listening to them, and clear about my desire to pause the conversation, it's always worked out well.

My final conclusions from these experiences is this: when someone feels truly listened to, they don't hold onto the conversation in the same way.

It's all about seeing and listening to the other person with clear presence; then, they will feel seen and heard, even for a brief moment. This is not a commitment for life; choosing this way of interacting takes less energy than pulling away or avoiding someone. In the end, both of you feel better.

Kindness is doing ordinary things with extraordinary love
~ Leunig

The eighth step to creating and living in a kinder world... being kinder with yourself and others...

Listening and intentional chit chat

In this section, you'll practice two things you can do to promote kindness, both involving momentary acknowledgment of another person.

To introverts who may consider these actions beyond their tolerance level; you don't have to do what I suggest here. There are a variety of ways you can generate more kindness. Be kind to yourself if this task feels too hard right now.

This goes for everyone. You can always choose when you want to do it. Remember, do this practice when you feel safe or ready, even if it's only once a day or once a week.

One of the safest places to experiment with full presence in listening is on the phone when you're speaking to a stranger from an airline, the phone company or a customer service help line.

Begin by asking the person on the other end of the line how they're doing that day. I do this frequently, and the most common response I hear is surprise in their voice as they thank me for asking. You may not be surprised to learn the conversations usually take an easier trajectory when they begin this act of kindness.

Here's your kindness task:

1. Throughout your day, whenever you find yourself in an interaction with a stranger, pause for a moment and ask them how they are. Give them your complete attention for a few moments. (Remember, you can practice this on the phone if it's easier). Observe how they respond. Do they brighten up a bit? Do they sound and feel a bit more human to you? How do you feel as you walk away (or hang up)? Did that little act of kindness appear to help both of you feel a little better?

2. The next time you run into a person in your life who usually over-demands your attention, take a deep breath, slow yourself down, and settle in to listen to them. Ask them questions as you listen, this can be short time span, a few minutes. It's okay at a certain point to look at your watch and say, "My apologies. I have to go now. It was nice chatting with you."

You will definitely see results from this over time. You will significantly increase the balance in your kindness account!

ask
love
words
unconditional
profoundness
kindness
care
creates
giving
confidence
thinking
caring
share
loving
purpose
sharing
donate
help
give
hope
community
please give

"Kindness in words creates confidence.

Kindness in thinking creates profoundness.

Kindness in giving creates love."

~ Lao Tzu

CHAPTER NINE

The Twins — Generosity and Kindness...

Whenever someone is talking about how kind another person is, they almost always use the same common phrase: "She is so generous...so kind." People often equate generosity to kindness. According to the dictionary definition below generosity and kindness appear the same.

Generosity
gen·er·os·i·ty [,jenə'räsədē]
noun

1. the quality of being kind and generous: *"I was overwhelmed by the generosity of friends and neighbors"*

Synonyms: liberality, lavishness, magnanimity, munificence, open-handedness, free-handedness, unselfishness, kindness, benevolence, altruism, charity, big-heartedness, goodness, bounteousness.

In turn, generosity can show up or be demonstrated in a variety of different ways. Being generous with our words, giving compliments, fosters kindness. Recent research shows how kindness in action has a larger, beneficial effect not only on ourselves, but also on the people around us, including people with whom we interact daily, at work, in the errands we do each day, interactions with family, friends and acquaintances.

A Harvard Business Review article "Don't Underestimate the Power of Kindness at Work" by Ovul Sezer, Kelly Nault, and Nadav Klein, gives an excellent description if the benefits of kindness in action.

> "A commitment to be kind can bring many important benefits. First, and perhaps most obviously, practicing kindness will be immensely helpful to our colleagues. ... Receiving a compliment, words of recognition, and praise can help individuals feel more fulfilled, boost their self-esteem, improve their self-evaluations, and trigger positive

emotions, decades of research have shown…

Second, practicing kindness helps life feel more meaningful. Being kind brings a sense of meaning because it involves investing in something bigger than ourselves. It shapes both how others perceive us — which improves our reputation — and how we view ourselves…

Third, as we found in a new set of studies, giving compliments can make us even happier than receiving them. … Consistently, we found that giving compliments actually made people happier than receiving them…

We found that giving compliments engendered a stronger social connection than receiving compliments because giving them encouraged people to focus on the other person. … Making a thoughtful, genuine compliment requires us to think about someone else — their mental state, behavior, personality, thoughts, and feelings. … In workplaces where acts of kindness become the norm, the spillover effects can multiply fast… In a landmark study analyzing more than 3,500 business units with more than 50,000 individuals, researchers found that acts of courtesy, helping, and praise were related … [to the] behaviors [that] were predictive of productivity, efficiency, and lower turnover rates. When leaders and employees act kindly towards each other, they facilitate a culture of collaboration and innovation. … [Additional] research finds that people appreciate small acts of kindness as much as large ones." [1]

Other ways you can be generous is with your home by sharing it with others, for meals, letting them stay over, storing things. You can be generous with your belongings, lending them or giving them to others. You can be generous with your time. One readily recognized way of being generous is with your money, giving gifts or making donations in meaningful ways to help others.

People often consider themselves as generous. Conversely, there are a few people who pride themselves of the opposite, of not being generous. What's strange is the people who think of themselves as generous or not generous are not necessarily seen the same way by other people. What accounts for this disparity? Beyond the wide range of beliefs on what constitutes generosity, this disparity presents a topic worth looking at.

Generosity is typically seen as a form of giving, and part of giving includes receiving. It may not appear obvious how giving and receiving can be two sides of the same coin, and yet, giving and receiving are related. The two parts make up the cycle of the whole.

The idea is complicated; consider anyone you know, including yourself, who is generous in giving, however, they are not generous with themselves when it involves receiving. This is remarkably similar to our exploration into the concept of giving and receiving kindness.

Then there's the distinction between receiving and taking. Just as giving and receiving are interrelated, so is giving and taking. Consider this, do you know a person(s) who gives to someone to justify taking from someone? Does this resonate with you?

Rarely, will anyone dispute generosity is held in high regard as a quality to have or see in another person. Additionally, it's believed true generosity is demonstrated through acts of giving; often, this is an accurate assessment—an act of generosity is truly an act of giving.

There are times, however, when an apparent act of generosity is not true giving. This disconnect is seen when a person gives in an attempt to demonstrate to others (and maybe even to the person who's doing the giving) how good a person they are. Occasionally, it's done for no other reason than to get something back. When the motive for giving comes from one of these reasons it reflects the self-interest of the person and their self-esteem or persona they wish to project, rather than expressing a true generous spirit.

Clearly, giving and generosity are complex themes. They can be colored and influenced by numerous factors, that can exist outside your awareness. It's not always easy to know when you're giving too much or giving too little.

I present to you a hypothesis; one I hope you can agree with. When you are generous, you feel good about it, and perhaps you feel good about yourself as well. This may be an obvious point; however, if you agree my hypothesis is accurate, then you already understand a good measure of what it means to be generous and can create more of it in your life.

It's time to get out your journal or a piece of paper or pad.

Write down your answers to the following questions:

1. **Where do you think you are generous in your life?**
   List as many (possible) ways and places, actual and possible, that you can think of. Include the little things, as well as the big things. It's easy to overlook the little ways in which you're generous.

2. **Who do you think of as a generous person?**
   How do they show it?
   Does every person on your list do it in the same way?
   What are some different ways they show their generosity?

3. **Are there any places in your life where you feel less generous?**
   Is it toward specific people and/or specific causes or differing events?
   How do you make those decisions?
   What factors do you consider?

4. **Are there places in your life where you felt or feel too generous?**
   In each of those places tell why it felt or feels like too much.
   When have you done this?
   How do you know it was too generous?
   What would it take to feel just right?

5. **Are there people, known to you, whom you do not consider generous?**
   How do they demonstrate their lack of generosity?

> Do they seem ungenerous 100% of the time, or only in certain contexts?
>
> 6. ***Are there people you know who are too generous?***
>   For each, what makes it feels like too much?
>   What are some of the different ways they do this?

The answers to these questions reveal a great deal about your values around generosity. They can serve as another baseline from which you can create more kindness. You will use them to explore how you may choose to expand your beliefs and actions regarding acts of kindness.

This doesn't necessarily mean you'll be upping your ante of giving. You may learn to be 'truly' generous by giving less!

Goldilocks giving to the three bears

The most truly generous persons are those who give silently without hope of praise or reward.
　　　　　　　　　~ Carol Ryrie Brink, "Caddie Woodlawn's Family"

I believe you know the fairytale about Goldilocks and the three bears. In it, a little girl named Goldilocks enters a bear family's cottage. In it she finds things that are too little, too large, or "just right." This story is a great tool for investigating your own relationship to generosity.

Now, imagine Goldilocks was giving gifts to the three bears for their birthdays.

To Papa Bear, the largest, she gave a pair of socks that had previously been given to her as a gift. Was the gift Goldilocks gave to Papa Bear a good gift?

On one hand, a gift is a gift, and we can believe it simply needs to be appreciated for being a gift. To be sure there's nothing wrong with re-gifting. Perhaps, her bear-friend loved the socks. On the other hand, though, she hadn't put a lot of thought into selecting it. It was something she had. What if the labels were no longer attached? Furthermore, Goldilocks may not have considered if her bear-friend wanted or needed socks, or if he'd like the color.

Was Goldilocks acting generously? You may answer, 'Yes, to a degree.' Did this expression of her generosity leave her with a good feeling? Perhaps yes, perhaps no. (We identified earlier that giving a gift will usually make one feel good.)

To the littlest bear she gave a birthday gift that was colossal. It was a huge, wide-screen TV. Though it was more than she was able to afford, she was certain her friend would love it. Besides everyone wants a big screen TV, right? Afterall, it was his birthday. Then, consider the next birthday, and the next? What does this mean for future birthdays? Will they need to be huge gifts also?

Perhaps, it was an anniversary birthday, 10, 20, 30, 40, 50, 65, or a special celebration birthday; still, the gift was huge, and probably over-the-top. Her bear-friend probably liked it a great deal, yet, maybe it also made him a bit uncomfortable. Possibly he is left with a sense of obligation that he's now required to give her a big gift on her birthday. Gifts that are too generous or go beyond the understanding of the level of the relationship can make people uncomfortable. Over-generous gifts can feel disproportionate to the event or to the relationship.

Another way to look at it… maybe… she gave this big gift to ensure he would like her more. If that's the case, who was the gift really for? Her, or her bear-friend? Or both? And did Goldilocks now have a satisfied feeling of generosity, of 'just right,' or was it more about how proud she felt for giving something so big?

The third birthday gift Goldilocks gave was to her bear-friend, Mama Bear. To her, she gave a frying pan, and not just any frying pan, either. This was an excellent, top-rated frying pan. She wished she could give her friend the whole set of pots and pans, yet it seemed it would be too much. She knew Mama Bear would love the pan because Mama Bear loved to cook; she had been talking about getting this exact pan the next time she had enough money and now she had it. It was exactly what Mama Bear wanted. It was 'just right.' Can you imagine the sense of satisfaction Goldilocks felt from giving a gift that was 'just right'?

Of course, you can't always know exactly what someone wants. In these three cases you can see, thought, how there are degrees of appropriateness for both the giver and the receiver. There is a sense of what feels 'just right.' Gift giving is only one way of being generous. It's a good one to look at as you investigate and understand your relationship to generosity and being kinder.

The bottom line is everyone has probably had all the different experiences in my Goldilocks birthday tale on both the giving and the receiving sides. If you stop and think about it, you can internally feel when it's either too small, too big, or just right when you give something. This 'just right' feeling extends beyond the feelings of the person you're giving the gift to; it also applies to what you, personally, feel comfortable in giving to the person.

Although we may think or feel a gift is to be appreciated as a gift, it doesn't prevent us from having difficult feelings when receiving a gift if it's too much or too little. These feelings are normal and are hard to ignore or pretend aren't there, regardless if we can't name why we feel the way we do. Key is being aware when it happens. You can't control what others give you; yet, at the same time, you, yourself, hold the power to take action on what and how you give and receive.

Think about it now. **How do you receive?**

> *For it is in giving we receive.*
> *~ Francis of Assisi*

If part of being generous and giving is also being able to receive, understanding how you receive a gift can give you insight into how you can be better at giving, be better at receiving and feel better about yourself.

Scientific reseach from J. V. Wood, S. A. Heimpel, L.A. Manwell and E. J. Whittington says when we have higher self-esteem and like ourselves more, we have the expectation life issues will frequently work out in our favor. It's stated that "...HSEs (High Self Esteems) have a greater sense of deserving positive outcomes in general and deserving positive moods than do LSEs (Low Self Esteems)"[2]

Specifically, we feel we deserve both positive outcomes and positive moods. Conversely, when we don't like ourselves and have lower self-esteem, we believe ourselves to be less worthy and less deserving.

The good news is there are steps you can take to bolster your ability to give and receive, and to strengthen your sense of feeling deserving.

Can you think of a time you had the experience of getting 'socks' as a gift (a tie? a bar of soap?). Did you say, "Oh, gee… thanks," then wonder what you will do with it?

Maybe you had negative thoughts about yourself or the other person: *Do I take such a gift as a measure of what they think about me, and feel bad about it; what does that say about them, their poor acknowledgment of me?*

Whether your first response is to wonder what you will do with the gift, if you choose to make it a measure of your self-worth, or if you make it a judgement of the giver; it's important to look past your feelings — to first and foremost appreciate a person has given you a gift. Take a moment to consider the act of gift-giving is of greater importance than the story you may choose to tell yourself regarding the gift itself and the intentions of the gift-giver.

Whenever you receive a gift from another person it signifies they wanted to give you something, regardless of the motivation. What you receive can have any number of factors behind it — they may not know what to get you, they may not know your tastes or they may not know your preferences… they cannot know if you can feel their intention behind it.

Feeling a sense of appreciation for the other person's act of giving is the highest state you can achieve when you receive a gift, whether you like it or not. It's possible to be grateful or appreciative for whatever you're given, regardless of what it is. A big one for me is, although I rarely eat sugar when someone gives me chocolate, I can genuinely thank them because I am grateful and appreciate they were thinking of me.

Going back to the conversation on feeling 'just right'. When you're given a gift that feels 'too much' can you describe what it was that evoked that feeling in you?

It's not always about the size of the gift. Frequently how you feel about yourself can affect your ability to accept a gift. Your comfort or discomfort can be a measure of your self-worth and what you feel you deserve. With this in mind, whenever you feel like something is too much, look into how you're feeling about yourself in that moment, this will include how you are in relationship to the person or people who gave you the gift.

Many years ago, a number of my friends got together and bought me a VCR for my birthday. (For those who don't know, a VCR was how we viewed videocassettes on a TV in the 1980s and 1990s. Yes, I am old!) This was no ordinary VCR, it was both hi-fi and stereo, a humongous deal. I can't remember ever being so moved or touched. My feelings bordered on overwhelming; I didn't know how to respond.

I'd never received a gift this monumental. When I received it, I had to evaluate my self-worth and shift something inside myself regarding my self-image. Did I like myself enough to deserve such a gift? Did it mean I am now obligated to give all of them grand gifts? That moment was eye-opening for me. It's still part of my personal story of giving and receiving.

You know the gifts that make you feel it's 'just right'. Occasionally it's an item you pointed out or mentioned, the person remembered and bought it for you. Othertimes it's an item you never saw before or thought about, yet it was something you know you'll use and like. It can be something that supports you in your life… in what you do or want to do more of: art supplies, sports equipment, a gift certificate to a spa.

In all of these cases, how you're able to receive is a measure of how you feel about yourself, and how worthy or deserving you may or may not think you are.

The other side of this coin is when you make the gift a measure of the giver; how generous they are, how stingy they are, or how thoughtful they are. A measure of understanding helps stop the judgement about the person if you can understand that one person can be better at choosing gifts than another person. It's a waste of your energy and time to judge or evaluate the act of giving of another person or yourself. You will never know the full story, either inside them or inside yourself.

Go back to the lists you made earlier in this in chapter, and add to your answers.

1. ***Where do you think you are generous in your life?***
   In each instance, when did it feel like too little, too much, or 'just right'?

2. ***Who do you think of as a generous person?***
   For each person, when do they do it too little, too much or 'just right'? Or is it the same each time?

3. ***Are there any places in your life where you feel less generous than you would like?***
   In each of these, what makes it feels like too little?
   What would it take to feel 'just right'?

4. ***Are there places in your life where you felt or feel too generous?***
   In each of those places, tell why it felt, or feels, like too much?
   What would it take to feel 'just right'?

5. ***Are there people you know who are not generous?***
   For each, what do they do that makes it feel like too little?
   What would it take to make it feel 'just right'?

6. ***Are there people you know who are too generous?***
   For each, what makes it feels like too much?
   What would it take to make it feel 'just right'?

Read through your first list of answers and see if you have a better understanding in reference to the values you have in regards to giving and receiving. Is your understanding more specific than when you thought about this before?

Be kind to yourself. This isn't about making changes today. Our intention is to deepen your awareness and understanding, this helps you recognize what causes the feelings you have when you give and receive.

Giving to get

Earlier in this chapter I mentioned three aspects of giving. The first was giving, pure and simple. The second is giving as an attempt to demonstrate what a good person you are (which is usually more about you). And the third is giving to get something back.

We all can relate to the first. In those times when our ego or a desire to look good gets in the way and our motivations get muddy, we can relate to the second. The third aspect of giving, as a means to get something back in return, is more insidious.

The underlying thinking may be this: *I know I deserve more than I have, if I give more, surely, I will get more.* Meaning, the size of the gift you give (and get) is how you measure yourself. And if you give a big gift, for sure you should get a big gift in return. This will then prove how loved or lovable you are.

This last form of giving can come from a feeling of lack. It operates in one's subconscious mind, is unbelievably tangled, and is difficult to unravel.

Maybe Goldilocks felt a sampling of these motives when she gave the big TV to her baby bear-friend. Whenever I have received gifts like this, it has made me feel uncomfortable.

At times, I knew the person who gave it didn't have the extra money for the pricey gift. Other times I felt uncomfortable because I thought it necessary to reciprocate in a similar manner. Probably the hardest for me, I felt the other's desire to be loved and suspected they were using that 'too big' gift as a measure of how lovable they were. Whether this was true or a projection of mine, I don't/didn't know. Either way, I found it hard.

I also know I've done the same thing. I always loved giving grand gifts, if the recipient said, "Oh, this is just too much!" it was wonderful. Indeed, I did take it as a measure of how lovable I was. I did this for many years, until I began to choose to look seriously into my motivations.

I'd love to say I have this particular aspect of giving mastered, yet, I'm still working on it. I can easily fall into this habit of tapping into my love of giving grand gifts without the awareness of the meaning it holds for me.

What helps me to stay in honest integrity with my motivation behind gift giving is looking for the 'just right' feeling or the sense the gift is 'just right' for the relationship.

To do this, it's important I answer these questions for myself:

First I ask: can I afford this grand gift? — asking myself later how I'll pay for the gift is not good or kind to myself. Thankfully, I can't disingenuously deprive myself of an enjoyable activity (i.e.: going out to dinner) for an extended period of time, to compensate for one moment of great giving.

It's important I consider how the other person will feel upon receiving my grand gift. Beyond the immediate pleasure of the person getting the gift, I need to consider how the person may feel in regards to me giving gifts to them. Of importance is to feel and look inside myself to know if I'm being motivated by a sense of my own self-worth, or by a sense of lack in myself. If I'm feeling lacking or needy in any way, I have to ask myself if I'm trying to ameliorate it through this misguided way of giving.

These are all difficult questions to ask and to accept the honest answer for ourselves. I offer them as your own guide. For me, I'm continually getting better at it. I know you will too, as you practice them.

Now, answer the questions below with a new focus.

1. **Where do you think you are generous in your life?**
   In any of these places, are you generous so you can get something back? If you are, are there underlying needs you are hoping to get met? What are they?
   Remember, no judgement. Be kind to yourself.

2. **Who do you think of as being generous?**
   When a person gives a gift to you or others, do you interpret their actions as coming from their own needs, rather than a true spirit of generosity?

Does it feel as if they want a reciprocal gift when they give? What makes you think that's true?

Again, these answers are to deepen your awareness and understanding. You may gain awareness of hidden or subconscious motivations you (or another) may have. When you increase your awareness and understand things on a new level, change is slowly possible over time.

Getting it 'just right'... *Heads or tails?*

Hopefully, your answers to the above questions helped you understand how you, as an individual, handle giving and receiving. Understanding this can bring you closer to getting it 'just right'. That feeling of 'just right' will speak to your thoughtfulness as the giver and help you make the distinctions needed to inform the choices you make.

In addition to the previous questions, I have yet another way to help me decide if my motivation for giving is 'just right'. Although a bit odd, this is an easy-to-use method, and it does work!

Think of a gift you may be thinking of giving someone and how 'right' it feels. Then, flip a coin. Heads means it's 'right,' and tails means it's 'not right.'

Here's the twist… while the coin is in the air and coming down, notice what you hope it will be? **Do not look at the coin the minute it lands!**

Notice what you were hoping for and do that thing, not what the coin shows. If you have any doubt in your mind, and you feel it's too much (or too little), you'll know it. If there's certainty, you'll know that, too. Either way, you'll act accordingly.

This technique also works with other decisions in which you feel conflicted.

Thus far we've discussed: the ideas you hold of generosity; the relationship you have to generosity; and your 'generosity' motivations for giving and receiving. In all of these examples that explore generosity — there is an unavoidable truth that can feel like a trap.

Life isn't like a fairy tale, or easy like flipping a coin. Every person's life has many complications, complexities, associations, and outcomes that can challenge a person to the core. Life happens, and there are issues that may be hard to navigate around or through them. The kindest gift you can give to yourself is being patient and being gentle with yourself as you explore all aspects of growing kinder through the years.

There are things you can begin to do right now to shift your relationship with generosity, and to practice more kindness toward others and yourself.

You cannot do a kindness too soon because you never know how soon it will be too late.
~ Ralph Waldo Emerson

The ninth step to creating and living in a kinder world... being kinder with yourself and others...

Being generous... to yourself and to others

1. **Practicing being generous by giving just a little bit more.**
   If you've ever had a job where your earnings were from tips, this will definitely resonate with you. Tip just a little bit more. A few places and ways it's easy to practice this are: after a meal in a restaurant, when you get you haircut, or when you take a taxi, Uber, or Lyft.

   For example, for every five dollars (or less) of a tip, add one dollar more. If your calculation says the tip is $3, give $4. If $10, give $12. If the tip comes to $20, give $24. I want to stress these amounts are a suggestion; only do it only if it's affordable to you. In any case, it's not the percentage or the amount that's important, it's that you are being intentionally more generous with giving. You're doing it with the motivation that you'll receive nothing in return from the person receiving the extra tip.

Be prepared for challenging internal conversations. I recently took friends to dinner and the bill came to $70.00. I usually tip 20%, which would be $14.00, bringing the total to $84.00. I had $90.00 in my wallet, and I decided to give the whole $90.00. To my surprise, the minute I had the thought to give all I had in my wallet, not just 20%, I had internal conflict. I thought, Is this too much? Should I do it? on and on. I ended up giving the full $90.00. As I left the restaurant the waitress stopped me and said, "You made my night!" Which made my night!

2. **Praise and acknowledgment** – Give a compliment and praise someone when you see them doing something well. Make it a habit

3. **Practice being kind to yourself** - This next process is open-ended; you decide how you want to do it.

Each week give yourself something, a gift. It can be extra money or extra time just for yourself. It can be allowing yourself the pleasure of doing one thing you like to do. Use your imagination.

Whatever you give yourself can change week to week, if you choose to do that.

Quick start ideas…

- put aside $15 to buy yourself something special
- save the $15 over several weeks to get something you've wanted for a while and didn't have the money.
- once a week treat yourself to a massage, a facial, or a shave.
- set aside time to go on a favorite hike or walk.

The important point is to practice this regularly, weekly when possible. Choose something that's affordable in terms of cost and/or time. Whatever you decide to do, make sure you do it!

It is to your immediate benefit to practice being more generous to yourself and to develop the practice until it becomes a habit.

In the exercises above you're practicing being kind to others and yourself in small, regular ways over a period of time that will add up to measurable shifts in how you give and receive.

4. **Do something kind for a someone you don't know directly -** You can do this in a multitude of ways. You may decide to donate to a cause or a non-profit. It can be a one-time donation or a recurring weekly or monthly donation. This can be a small amount; every dollar donation adds up, don't reject the amount as too small!

Alternatively, you may give your spare change to a person on the street asking for help. I recently had a credit in a store where I don't usually shop. I chose something in the store for myself, and I still had $15 left. I wandered around looking for a way to spend that remaining $15 credit without any luck at finding or thinking of anything I wanted or needed. I approached a young person looking at jackets and gave the credit to him. I wish I had a picture of the smile on his face. Perhaps you can imagine the smile on my face, as well!

PART FOUR
Going Deeper with the Practice of Kindness

"This is what is hardest:

to close the open hand

because one loves."

~ Friendrich Nietzsche

CHAPTER TEN

Tough Love, A Good Thing

Kindness is often mistakenly seen as synonymous with being nice, saying yes to everything, or saying yes to everything to make everything okay for everybody. It can be all these things, yet, when it's only about these behaviors, it can turn out to be not kind to either ourselves or others.

Being kind includes creating boundaries and involves knowing whether it's kinder to ourselves or the other person to say 'Yes' or to say 'No'. Saying no is not easy for most people; our natural response is to please others and to be liked. Plus, saying no runs the risk of angering or disappointing someone, and perhaps being rejected. Too often it's easier to say yes or simply give in, rather than face an uncomfortable moment.

In his book, *"Compassion Focused Therapy: Distinctive Features"*, Paul Gilbert writes:

> "…compassion is not about submissive "niceness" — it can be tough, setting boundaries, being honest and not giving clients what they want but what they need. An alcoholic wants another drink — [and this] is not what they need, many people want to avoid pain and may try to do so in a variety of ways — but [kind] clarity, exposure and acceptance may be what actually facilitates change and growth."[1]

Sometimes saying no is the clear choice, and you're acting in the best interest of both others and yourself when you respond to a request or invitation with a no. In one of my professional training programs, a trainee offered what she thought was a great idea. I listened to her proposal and said "No." She was completely taken aback. To her, it was a great idea! With my broader perspective and experience, I understood her idea would create numerous difficulties further on. By saying 'no,' I was protecting her and others from future unnecessary challenges. She said, "I thought this work was about being flexible!" I responded that she was right… "and sometimes I'm flexible enough to know when and how it's advisable not to be flexible."

I wasn't harsh in my response. I spent more time with her, explained the complications that could result from her idea. In the end, she understood. I suspect one of the best things that came out of our conversation was that she saw seeing how 'no' was a viable choice, one of many.

If 'no' doesn't exist as a choice for you, you're left with 'yes,' which is no choice, at all… especially when you know it's not the best answer. The outcome is you are being unkind to yourself, and often, you are being unkind to others.

Mirroring life, saying yes or no isn't always a black and white choice. There are approximations with a 'no' or a compromise.

A therapist friend of mine told me a story that's a great example of a mother being kind to both herself and her child.

My therapist friend, Jane (not her real name), was visiting her friend who had a three-year-old girl. The little girl came into the room where the two women were and asked for M&M candies. Her mother told her "No," that it was too close to dinner and the candy would ruin her appetite. The little girl, being three, was unable to see the logic in her mother's explanation and went into a temper tantrum. The mother quickly compromised, putting the tantrum to rest by saying, "Okay, you can have three M&M's."

The little girl was happy, and the mother ended the tantrum without concern her daughter wouldn't eat her dinner. It was a win-win in both the little girl's eyes and her mother's.

Jane, the therapist, saw it differently. "I can't believe you let her manipulate you like that," she said. "You gave into her!"

Her friend came back with the perfect response. "Jane, she has to learn there are some battles in life she can win. What she doesn't know is, right now, I am choosing which ones she wins."

I love this story. It illustrates quite well an approximation to 'no,' which means almost, but not quite no. This story demonstrates the mother's concern for her child's well-being. The mother knew her own priorities. She made sure her child ate well and took care of herself in the process of compromising. In sum, a bit of kindness all around.

You can well imagine how the scene would've played out with the three-year-old girl having an extended, full-fledged tantrum if her mother had flatly said, no. I don't have children myself. I'm an 'uncle' to many of my friends' kids. What I know, though, is I can promise if her mother had given in and said yes, she would've had a child charged up with sugar late in the day, with no appetite for dinner. As a result, neither of them would've been happy.

Perhaps you can recall a moment when you knew you were doing the kind thing, although it may have been difficult. Maybe this difficult 'kind' action was with a child, as in the story above; perhaps it was at work, letting someone know the job they did was not done well. Certainly, these may be hard conversations to have, yet in the end, they are kinder conversations; because it is much better — and kinder — than misleading someone or not putting a child's well-being first.

The Truth

I have a hard time with the word Truth; as I'm not sure what the truth is in any given circumstance or belief system. Whenever I hear someone begin a sentence with "The truth is…", I back away, concerned with what may follow. I respond similarly if a sentence begins with the words 'in fact,' or 'actually.' When I hear myself saying these words, I do my best to backtrack and say what I want to say another way.

I've encountered many people who tell the truth; frequently 'the truth' is offered without asking permission, other times 'the truth' is verbalized as criticism. When I can sense the person(s) is honestly showing concern for me and interest in me when they say what they see; I am able to appreciate it, as I realize it's about their truth, and the facts as they know them.

Remember this, every person has an internal sense of what they mean by 'the truth.' A large number of people believe speaking 'the truth' is keyed into reality without considering whose reality they are keyed into. Knowing this, you may wonder when it makes sense to share what you see as 'the truth,' whether it can be a kind thing to do, or whether it can be an unkind thing to do.

A gift from my mother

My mother, who was a painter, died when she was 54; when I was 22 and my brother was 20. As we were going through her effects we found letters she'd written to us fifteen years earlier. When my mother, at age 39, wrote the letters, my brother was five and I was seven years old.

In reading the letters, we learned she had wanted to tell us things we were too young to understand at the time she wrote them. I imagine she wrote these things down when she did because her mother had died at the age of 39, and these thoughts were on her heart. Perhaps she wrote them when she did in case she didn't survive until we were old enough to understand.

Her words gave me, taught me, the best measure for me to use when I choose to speak *my truth*.

Here is the letter my mother wrote:

Dear Children,
I write this as I am approaching 39. This is the age when my mother died. At the time, I was 19, and 39 seemed centuries away. I have not the slightest intention of leaving you for still 'many centuries,' if God will agree. If, however, this were the midnight of my life, I would like to tell you certain things. I mentioned God and truly I don't know if I believe in him or not. I choose to think I do. When I was your age, I thought I saw him in the shape of a cloud, now, I think it again, in rather a different way. There is so much beauty in a cloud, such momentary grandeur, it well may be a Godly thing. There is only one thing remains constant to me. That is beauty. I hope one day you can feel the exhilaration of a beautiful picture, a beautiful moment, a beautiful thing. Now beauty, my dear boys, is not always pretty. It is very often ugly. But it is pure.
This brings me to another important point. To be able to judge the pure from the impure, the true from the fake, you must first be able to be true to yourself. This takes a very long time. When it does, a new world opens within and you are free of the pangs of guilt and remorse. This truth of which I speak is a kind of Godliness again. It is never our intention to hurt, but if one day the truth to yourself causes hurt to someone else, think twice. And

> *if after you have wrangled with your conscience, and are sure you are not creating a greater lie within you, then, and only then, dare you cause pain. Although you will find the idea not original with me, truth and beauty (and a reasonable amount of pleasantness!) are indeed God and Godliness.*

I have thought long and hard about her words since I first read the letters. I'm still not sure it is the 'truth' for me. It's taken time over the years for her ideas to resonate inside me in ways that feel more and more true. Especially these lines:

> *It is never our intention to hurt, but if one day the truth to yourself causes hurt to someone else, think twice. And if after you have wrangled with your conscience, and are sure you are not creating a greater lie within you, then, and only then, dare you cause pain.*

Although these words can usually be applied when it's clearly kinder not to tell the truth to avoid hurting another person unnecessarily; it also applies when the situation necessitates that I speak up to ensure I am being kind to myself. As difficult as it is for me when I'm at the challenging crossroad of 'to speak' or 'not to speak'; it helps to have a criterion to direct me to withhold speaking to avoid hurting a person, and for speaking to make sure I do not hurt myself.

What my mother wrote was, and is, tremendously meaningful to my brother and I. She was not religious, yet, she unmistakably had a deep spiritual nature and was a thoughtful person. I think my brother and I are, as well. Although our mother died young, my brother and I were fortunate to experience her honesty, and for the gift of her 'truth' that she brought into our lives.

Tough love, a good thing

Navigating difficult situations around telling what you see as the truth can be tricky. I once found myself in a dilemma while teaching that has become good example of a successful navigation with one's truth.

As an Educational Director of Feldenkrais Professional Training Programs, I teach and oversee all my trainees over the course of their four years of study. My charge is to ensure they're ready to be practitioners when they finish.

There are multiple training programs worldwide, and at times, people make up time they missed in their own programs by coming to one of mine. My responsibility towards these people is different than with my regular trainees. I am not responsible for deciding or evaluating their readiness to graduate and become a Feldenkrais® Practitioner. That responsibility lies with the Educational Director in their own program. This was the case with Mary (not her real name).

Mary attended one of my programs for a month. She left to return to her own program and then came back to make up an additional month. At this point I said to her, "With the amount of time you are making up here, it may have been better if you had transferred to my training."

By the end of her third month with me, with her making up time missed in her own program, she had theoretically reached the point where she could graduate. Since I felt she wasn't yet ready to work as a practitioner; I had a problem. I was in a quandary. I wasn't sure what to do.

Should I inform her Educational Director? Should I tell her? What was my responsibility, both professionally and personally? In the end, I concluded it was not my responsibility. It was the responsibility of her Educational Director. I let it go.

However, the truth for me was… I couldn't let it go.

On the day she fulfilled her make-up requirements, I asked her to have coffee with me. Mary was distinctly nervous when we sat down, perhaps a part of her knew something was up.

"Are you going to drop a bomb on me?" she said.

"No" I replied. "Yet, I do think we are going to have a difficult conversation."

I shared my dilemma regarding where the responsibility for her advancement lay; I asked Mary if it was her Educational Director's responsibility or my responsibility to evaluate her. I said I had a responsibility to be honest with her, noting that I didn't want her to be misled or to be unprepared for anything she wasn't ready for. Continuing the conversation, I said, "my concerns come from a professional perspective. I don't think you are ready to graduate; you need more experience, additional practice and further instruction."

This was a difficult conversation. It would've been easier to let it go. I could have told myself it was not my job. Whether it was or wasn't my job was not the important aspect; I felt a personal level of responsibility, one person to another.

I dreaded this conversation and was concerned how she might respond. As I feared, she was defensive and angry with me, at first. She asked if I was going to report her or try to interfere with her graduation. I assured her I wouldn't do either; I reiterated that my sole intention was speaking in her best interest, for her to have honest feedback from me since she had been training with me.

The nugget I want you to get, is this, I didn't say she couldn't practice the Feldenkrais Method®. I stated what I thought she could do to become better able to practice it. I recommended that she practice the Feldenkrais Method® consistently on clients without charging money for the next two years; and that she visit other training programs to further her learning.

In the end, I felt I'd done the right thing, for her and for me. It definitely felt like tough love.

The good news… she did what I recommended. She continued to visit one of my other programs; at one point she told me she was grateful for my honesty and she said I helped her towards her goal.

At the beginning of this chapter, I discussed the challenges of creating more kindness by setting boundaries with saying either yes or no to someone. Importantly your choices are arrayed on a continuum we may label "Creating More Kindness through Tough Love." As in the example with Mary, tough love can be a hard thing to give. Learning to be truly honest, to tell your truth to both others and yourself, can take time, skill, and practice.

The only way you learn to get better speaking your truth with kindness is by doing it in every single opportunity that calls for it. Practicing it is the bottom line. In time you will see tough love as truly an act of kindness.

Tough love may not be easy; however, it comes from a desire to care about both another person and yourself. Tough love is fundamental to being a kinder person.

Tough love is about you, too

There's a misconception that tough love is something you only give to someone else. Did you think that was true? Tough love is something you give to yourself, as well… and can be tougher to engage with yourself than it is to engage with another person.

The deal with being tough with yourself is you often head in the other direction when you feel that what is coming up can be tough. You may do your best to avoid it; calling this response a solid self-protective mechanism. But is it self-protection or something else? Most people tend to avoid situations for which they feel unprepared and unskilled. Navigating difficult situations falls into this realm. As with anything, the ONLY way you gain proficiency in the arena of tough love is to engage and practice it.

Tough love is always a choice; it's important to have a way of knowing *when* you might engage.

Consider a time you've had an interaction with someone that never felt resolved. The interaction was probably a difficult situation and you chose to let it go. You told yourself it wasn't important or didn't matter. You told yourself you really didn't care about it; letting it go felt easier than dealing with it.

Letting it go is a common response; most people don't want to have a difficult encounter with another person if they can avoid it.

Another common response can happen after you let it go; you continue to think about it, maybe not all the time, then, something triggers it, a loop starts running in your head and the same unresolved feelings rise up.

In the words of my mother:

> *It is never our intention to hurt, but if one day the truth to yourself causes hurt to someone else, think twice. And if after you have wrangled with your*

> *conscience, and are sure you are not creating a greater lie within you, then, and only then, dare you cause pain.*

The part we're visiting now is the second sentence.

> *And if after you have wrangled with your conscience, and are sure you are not creating a greater lie within you…*

"Wrangling with your conscience." This may be that recurring internal conversation running a loop in your mind, where you relive the incomplete moment or conversation. Let's go back to my phrase for endless negative and counter-productive thoughts I shared in Chapter Five, *driving around in a bad neighborhood*. This time, instead of just getting the hell out of there, *park the car and do something about it*.

Sound tough? You bet it is. Because in nearly all instances you'd rather pretend the difficult conversation or mistake you made that needs fixing, or whatever that thing is that's bedeviling you, is not there. If it's still unresolved and bothering you, it's denial. If you can add all the minutes and energy you spent rehashing it, dealing with feelings, telling the story to others; again, it's denial. The unresolved conversation becomes a weight you carry around without realizing how heavy it's become. I know; I've been there more than once.

It doesn't have to be this way. You can do something about that conversation or thing bedeviling you. You will feel lighter, better, happier, and kinder to yourself when you address what's unresolved. I know, because it happened for me, and for people like Mary, the trainee in my program I felt wasn't ready to graduate.

My challenge with Mary turned into a nagging thought after I first decided to let it go. Then it became a distraction, that lasted only a moment or two, but always came back. I'm confident it would still be coming back today, have me wrangling with it, if I had never spoken with her.

You're probably like me, having enough on your mind that you'd rather not be reminded by these sorts of things. It's hard to avoid, though. How often does someone's name come up and you immediately go into a 'story' about them. As human beings, we think and relate in stories. So, if you see a name somewhere, you might dwell on it for a minute. If it's while talking with another person, you might interrupt to recount the entire story, again. I bet you can think of times this has happened, right?

There are two things you can do to break the pattern.

The first is to truly let it go. Your success letting it go will only show up when the person, incident, or conversation no longer comes up in your internal conversations, or when you don't retell the story at the mere mention of the person. You'll rest easier and move on when you see you've released it.

The second thing to do is attend to the irritation by acting on it. Perhaps you call the person involved and ask for a conversation. Or maybe discuss it with someone else — a friend, or professional — to help you move on.

This is what tough love is. It's tough to acknowledge to yourself the issue is still unresolved, it's even tougher to act on it for any possible resolution, and it's being kind to yourself when you do.

One thing to remember is that acting in this way won't guarantee you'll get the outcome you desire, especially if it involves another person or relationship. It's great when you get your desired outcome, and I assure you it's also great if you don't. You will have greater clarity regarding your relationship; you will know you did what you could to help bring yourself and the situation to a better place. What must be present is your willingness to find out, your willingness to see where the conversation leads. Keep reminding yourself you're engaged in an act of kindness to both yourself and to them.

It's worth repeating that most people often don't often act because they have not done whatever it is that needs doing enough to be skilled at it. The one thing that's true for everyone is you have to begin somewhere.

A few things to remember as you move forward.

One, every suggestion I give you won't work all the time. Circumstances, people, relationships, place, time… there is always a new twist.

Two, there are times you're going to feel unprepared for that twist.

Three, be willing to venture into the unknown and discover what's possible. You're moving toward love and kindness when you do.

While I can never be sure how someone will respond to what I say, I've learned what words work best leading into a difficult conversation, and what words don't work well, at all.

What doesn't work are these phrases or similar ones:

- We need to talk.
- We better have a conversation.
- Do you think we need to talk?
- I am tired of carrying this around in me.
- I am upset with you.
- I've been having feelings for a while now.

There are a multitude of variations of the above. These phrases will place a person on the defensive, and a difficult conversation will become harder when that happens.

What often *works better:*

- Can we find a time to talk? There are some things I would like to talk with you about.
- I would like to have a conversation with you. It might be a bit awkward.
- This might be an awkward conversation
- This might be a difficult conversation.
- This is a difficult conversation for me.
- I keep having a conversation with you in my head, and think it would be better if we had it for real.

While you can't know how the person will respond, these questions convey more of a sense of inviting them rather than confronting them. You're looking for an opening where a conversation can begin.

I also recommend you have these conversations in person when possible. The phone is your second-best choice.

Do not do it over e-mail or text; your intentions and meaning can be misunderstood in emails and texts. Rarely do we know what tone our written words convey, and how another person may interpret the words they read. The importance of the other person hearing your voice and you hearing their voice, cannot be overstated. Also, the immediacy of setting a misunderstood phrase right is paramount, which you can do when you're in each other's presence.

The Tenth Step to creating and living in a kinder world... being kinder with yourself and others...

Conversations

1. Think of someone you believe would appreciate an honest conversation with you, and benefit from it. Choose someone you feel comfortable approaching to give feedback and suggestions on how they might improve and better themselves. It's important how you do this, as it can be tricky.

2. Start by looking for a moment where they express a need or deep desire to understand or change something about themselves. Then ask them if they are interested or if it's okay to give them feedback. As I said, this can be sensitive. You don't want to put them off, if they aren't open or ready, let it go. Practice doing this in your imagination, which will shift something in how you understand and interact with them. AND, there may be another opportunity later when they are open to it. Just remember, it's always important how you begin the conversation. Keep reminding yourself you are doing this as an act of kindness to yourself and also to them.

3. Identify a 'conversation' you repeatedly have with yourself that loops over and over through your mind. It can be an event or another person. Decide what you want to do about it.

Can you let it go? Or is it something that needs to be dealt with? If you decide it needs to be dealt with, make the time to approach the person for a conversation, even if it feels challenging. Be willing to **find out if it can be resolved.**

Remind yourself you're doing this as an act of kindness to yourself and to them.

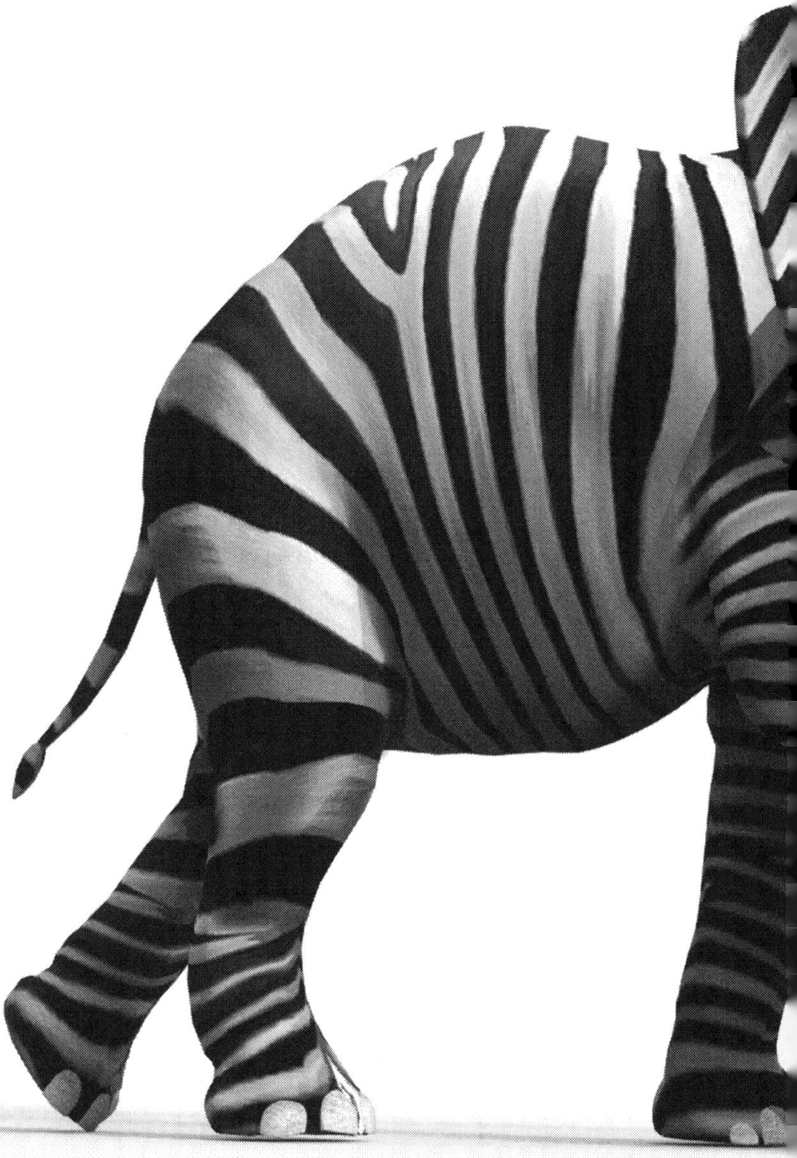

"Nothing is permanent about our behavior patterns except our belief they are so."

~ Moshe Feldenkrais

CHAPTER ELEVEN

Change Your Perspective, Change Your Life
Kindness Depends on How You See Things

Dr. Feldenkrais had an unusual and unique way of teaching. The first day he thoroughly presented an idea to help us understand it. The next day he presented the same idea from an opposite point of view. Usually, I was convinced this second way he presented the ideas was the more accurate and correct way of understanding it. On the following day, he presented the material a third time from an entirely new point of view. Each of his presentations was completely convincing, by the third day I was utterly and entirely confused. I didn't know which was the right way!

Eventually, I came to understand what he was doing, and why he chose this method of teaching. Dr. Feldenkrais' teaching methodology can be distilled down to two points of view. First, there is no one right way to look at an idea or concept; truly understanding anything required the consideration of many different, influencing factors. Secondly, each of us must learn to think for ourselves and not take an 'expert's' fact as 'fact'.

I'm inviting you to take this approach with this book. ***Nothing I say here is The Truth!*** Find what resonates for you, especially in each time you encounter a new idea. Question the concepts and viewpoints I present and draw your own conclusions.

It's about how you see things

You are probably one of the many who want to grow and change, you want to be the best possible version of yourself. It's a beautiful thing. The only catch is, are you going about your potential growth in all the wrong ways?

Kwong Roshi, a Zen teacher I had from the Sonoma Mountain Zen Center in California said, "we can view our desire to change as an act of aggression towards ourselves." This is a powerful statement I've never forgotten.

Think of the language you commonly use, look at the desire behind the words to eliminate an element that's part of you, as if that part is an enemy. Examples of this language are: "I hate ____ about myself; I want to get rid of ____; if only I could change ____."

What would you say if you found out you can't get rid of any parts of yourself? Everything that is you now will always be you, unless you experience a catastrophic event like brain damage. Yet, if a person experiences a major loss of mind or body, their biological and lived history remains a determinant of who they are. What this means is, any period of your life when you've experienced predominantly negative thoughts, feelings, and behaviors, the pattern stays within you. You will still have the capacity to experience the same or similar thoughts, feelings and behaviors again — regardless of whether you believe you've moved past them and things have changed. The difference between then and now is you may be able to interrupt them sooner, or not dwell on them as long, despite them still dwelling inside you.

I've witnessed this phenomenon surface with different types of physical pain. For example, a person who believes they've "gotten rid of" their back pain, then, it recurs in times of stress. They may deal with it better, and come out of it faster, though it hasn't completely gone from their body.

Take heart. This isn't bad news. This is a part of understanding a dimension of yourself that can help you move forward on your journey of expressing more kindness for yourself.

Although your desire to change your unlikeable aspects of yourself appears constructive, in reality, wanting to work hard to eliminate it may increase your attachment to the unlikeable aspects through your thoughts and actions.

We attach ourselves to what we want to get rid of

When you decide you dislike something or want to do away with it, you become bound to that thing without realizing it.

For example, choose an object in the room you're in, such as a chair. The chair will be a metaphor for a part of yourself you don't like.

Take a moment to imagine your dislike for this chair. Your first action is to move it far away from you, perhaps into another room or your garage. You move it because you don't want that chair anywhere nearby. It's out of sight and you think you're free of it.

What will trip you up, though, is since you know where you put it, every time you come close to where it is, you'll think about it. You'll feel its presence in a distinct way, you'll feel nervous or worried; to ensure you don't get anywhere near it, you have to know where it is all the time. You may think about it when it's far away from you; when you are on a plane headed to another city. Since you always know where it is, if you think about it randomly, you stay attached and connected to it.

This is no different than when you are trying to get rid of a part of yourself. The more you attempt to ignore something about yourself, the more you give it part of your attention. Anyone who has gone on a diet, understands how this works: you want to decrease the amount of food you eat; so, what do you think about constantly? Food!

Unlike an old chair you can dispose of, you can't dispose of the parts of who you essentially are.

If getting rid of what you don't want won't work; there is a solution to living with it.

This may feel counter-intuitive… the solution is learning to accept all of yourself without judgement, including all your traits and characteristics. When you do, it's possible to look at them differently, and embrace them to help you incorporate them into your self-image.

I hold onto a basic viewpoint: *we all did the best we could…with the information we had… at the time when we learned to act in a particular way.*

Let this be your viewpoint, too.

At one point, whatever you learned about who to be and what to do made a certain kind of sense. With what you knew and understood at the time, it may have even been the most sense you could make of your situation. Whether it was right or wrong doesn't matter. It was the best you could do.

Every time you encounter one of the traits or aspects about yourself you don't like, use the encounter as an opportunity to practice self-kindness.

Psychologists Neff and Germer, in their article "A Pilot Study and Randomized Controlled Trial of the Mindful Self-Compassion Program" state:

"Self-kindness refers to the tendency to be caring and understanding with oneself rather than being harshly critical. When noticing some disliked aspect of one's personality, for example, the tone of language used to acknowledge the shortcoming is kind and supportive. Rather than attacking and berating oneself for not being 'good enough,' the self is offered warmth and unconditional acceptance (even though particular behaviors may be identified as unproductive and in need of change)."[1]

> Take a moment now to think of some behavior you have you aren't especially fond of.
>
> Can you trace it back to when it began?
>
> Did this behavior actually make sense at the time?
>
> Did it serve you in some way?
>
> Did it fulfill some need or help you in a particular situation?

Whether you can see where it began or not, all your traits and characteristics — including those you most wish you could change — have somehow become a part of who you essentially are today. Self-kindness is remembering you did the best you could with what you had, and not judging yourself for it. Importantly, while you may not be able to imagine how or when it could possibly happen, these very same traits and characteristics may serve you again one day.

Grow

"Even though the future seems far away, it is actually beginning right now."
~ Mattie Stepanek

As my Zen teacher Roshi Kwong reminds us, wanting to change *can be seen as an act of aggression toward ourselves,* or in a simpler word, unkind. Let's look at the possibility there's a part of yourself you know no longer serves you. It can be a habit or a particular way of acting or thinking. Perhaps there's a better way to approach this part of yourself; a less violent way, a way that is kinder and gentler on yourself, a way that helps you like yourself more.

Instead of focusing on trying to eliminate something, the idea is to add something new to who you are. This involves a process of growing and/or evolving yourself until the newer aspects of who you desire to be eventually outweigh who you were when you liked yourself less.

Here's a visual to illustrate the concept. The shape below represents you. Imagine everything already in or about you fits into this shape.

You...

Now, imagine you grow and develop over time until you look more like this:

More you...

What's different between the two is all the things that made up your essential Self initially, are only half of who you are after you grew and developed over time. They all still exist as a part of you, and yet they're no longer all of you.

Go further into the future, as you continue to grow and evolve, you become more and more of who you want to be, and "YOU" looks like this:

Even more You...

All the aspects and traits that were initially you are now only one-third of who you are now, which means the things you wanted to get rid of occupy a much smaller percentage of who you are.

As you continue to grow and evolve, the initial part becomes a smaller and smaller portion of you!

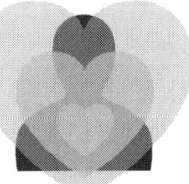

All of you... so far...

Observe, the initial You is still the same size! You didn't get rid of a thing!

Let's look at a few examples of what this can look like. If you are not happy with your diet, it doesn't mean you need to change everything about what and how you eat all at once. If you eat too much sugar, you can begin by replacing sugary snacks with fruit. Initially this will change how you shop and what you buy, later you can learn to cook delicious desserts where you can control the sweetness. Before long, you are spending your time differently, you are researching recipes, you are increasing the time you spend cooking; literally, you are feeding yourself in a different way.

Perhaps you spend too much money on clothes, or maybe you discover you don't always wear the new clothes you bought. Don't just throw them all away. If you do that you might end up with an empty closet only to refill it again with the same clothes you don't wear. Begin instead, by finding one item in your wardrobe you like, then, look for a new item to compliment the article of clothing you like.

Now is your chance to eliminate one item in your closet. Over time you will have replaced the clothing you don't wear; at the same time, you will have learned what you truly like and you will understand more about how to shop.

As you can see, both of these examples suggest making changes over time. These changes evolve along with your understanding of how you're doing what you do. You don't have to completely eliminate sugar from your diet, nor do you need to toss all your clothes. You can add to who you are, rather than getting rid of something that is already you.

Perspective is important.

Realistically, changes in who you are don't happen overnight. Looking at your growth and development through this lens of understanding can offer breathing space for how you change.

Everything you do in this book is part of cultivating and nurturing yourself to grow and develop in ways noted in the diagrams. As the diagrams show, this method contributes to that growth. If you consider new actions, and consistently engage in the practice of kind actions; you will grow, and positive change will occur. As time goes on, you'll discover the parts of yourself you currently dislike are smaller in relation to all of who you've become.

And kindness will flourish.

Going toward something, or moving away

A question to explore when you want to eliminate discomfort or make changes within yourself, is this; which direction do you choose to act from? You can move toward something, or away from it. The choice, toward or away makes a difference.

Usually when wanting to eliminate discomfort, or change a thing within themselves, people choose to get away from what they don't want. The common answers I receive when asking people what they want to improve about themselves, involves what they don't want: "I wish I weren't so lazy; I don't want to feel so tense; I should get another job." All are reasonable desires; underlying each is the assumption that once these changes happen, they will feel better about themselves. This could be true, but there's more to it.

Each one of these desires has one thing in common - the attempt to 'get away' from the thing they don't like, as in the metaphor of the distasteful chair I used earlier. Whatever they don't want, will still be there... unless they change their approach.

Instead, chose to move towards something you do want.

My uncle once asked me to work with him to eliminate a persistent pain he had in his lower back. He was a dentist and he attributed the pain to his work because he was constantly twisting to one side as he leaned over people.

He experienced relief from his pain at the end of each of our sessions. Yet, by the time I saw him the following week, it was back. After a few weeks going back and forth in this manner with the pain, I wanted to find a more enduring solution. During our next session, I thought of something different. I asked him, "You like to play golf, don't you?" His response was an enthusiastic "Yes!"

I asked if there was anything he wanted to improve on his golf game. He came up with several ideas, consequently, I took a completely different approach to treating him.

Instead of trying to help him 'get away' from his back pain, the focus became how he could 'go toward' improving his golf game. To improve his golfing, he had to learn to use his back differently. Taking this new approach, of coming from a different direction, to address the issue, his back pain disappeared completely. The change in perspective made the difference.

> Take a moment now to consider what direction you typically take when you think of changing something in yourself.
>
> Are you are trying to 'get away' from it?
>
> If so, can you switch it around to see yourself moving toward something, instead?

What you choose to move toward can be anything, as long as it interests you or brings you pleasure. Always make it something you look forward to; perhaps you will like yourself more for doing it.

Big picture... little picture

Many years ago, I saw a great film at the Smithsonian Air and Space Museum called *Powers of Ten*.2 Based on a book, *Powers of Ten: A Book About the Size of Things in the Universe and the Effect of Adding another Zero*,3 the film opens on a scene of a couple having a picnic in a park, shot from one meter away. The camera begins to zoom out from the scene until viewers can see the whole park the picnickers are in. It continues to zoom out, moving further and further away, each time increasing the distance by ten times until it's 10 to the 24th power (1024) away.

First, the viewer sees the whole park, then the entire city, on and on, until finally, the entire Milky Way Galaxy is in view.

Next, the camera reverses direction to zoom back toward the picnic scene. The camera zooms closer and closer in until the man's hand is in view, down to the details of his skin. It continues to zoom in until 10 to the minus 16th power (10-16), and the particles inside of protons are visible.

I was awed by the film. It was the first time I had any inkling of the power of perspective to affect experience. I became fascinated with the concept of perspective, particularly in how perspective might influence my thinking.

An event that happened to me years after I saw the film may be an example that's clearer to understand.

I suffered from a bad case of psoriasis, (happily, it's gone now.) At the time, it bothered me immensely and I went to a homeopathic practitioner to treat it. When homeopathic doctors and practitioners treat you, in addition to considering the condition you came to them for, they also consider other aspects of your life. Therefore, my first visit involved a comprehensive interview.

This happened during a time when I was thinking of leaving my private Feldenkrais practice to go into business with my brother who had just created a new invention of making metallic tiles. When this topic came up in the interview, the homeopath asked me two interesting questions in relation to this possibility:

I didn't have to think long on the first question. I told him the best that could happen is we would be a great success; in a few years we would sell the company for millions of dollars and be rich.

The second question was harder to answer. I had to think about it for a while. I started to answer my brother and I would stop talking with each other. Then I stopped myself, "No, the worst that could happen would be if one of us would kill the other."

Yikes!

I completely shocked myself with this answer. It was so extreme. I loved my brother. How could I have such a thought? And yet, it was true. That was the worst I could imagine happening.

The effect of that startling revelation, that one of us would kill the other, made the possibility of our not talking anymore seem mild and benign in comparison. What I had initially thought was the most terrible thing possible took on a completely different meaning when I stepped back and viewed it from a broader perspective.

This change in perspective helped me clarify what I wanted to do. I decided to begin a new Feldenkrais Training Program instead of going into business with my brother. Since then, both of us have gone on with our work quite successfully. I happily continued in my work, and one of the results is writing this book.

Too often, constraining yourself with your ideas about what might happen, good or bad, can lead to feelings and thoughts that perpetuate a negative way of seeing yourself. It can keep you stuck where you are and stop you from taking action in any direction.

I now use the same questions the homeopathic practitioner used with me when I talk with people who feel stuck or trapped.

What is the best that can happen? What is the worst that can happen?

These two questions offer them the chance to consider their options from both perspectives and helps them see the bigger picture. Plus, they get a greater understanding of where they are in their lives, which frequently opens them to insights they didn't see previously. Consequently, they gain clarity regarding what they want to create in their lives, and this clarity includes seeing what they don't want in their lives.

Changing perspective opens doors to greater self-understanding. Through greater self-understanding, you develop the capacity to generate more kindness toward others and yourself.

Step eleven to creating and living in a kinder world... being kinder with yourself and others...

Going toward something and shifting your perspective

1. Make a list of all of the things you want to change in your life. Take time to look over your list.

Notice how many of the things on your list are what you're trying to get away from. Now, rewrite your list from the perspective of what you want to go towards.

For example, if you wrote:

- I want to quit my job.

- I hate living in this city.

- My clothes are all out of style.

- I am too fat... too skinny... too... ???

See how you can turn them into statements that move you toward what you want, similar to these:

- I want to work in a more creative environment.

- I want to live in the country.

- I would love to wear something more stylish.

- I would like to develop healthier eating habits.

Remember, when you shift from 'getting away' to 'going towards', — the change will take time. Most change happens in a series of shifts inside you, a little at a time.

A successful strategy may offer these options:

- If you want a more creative job and can't quit your current one right away, you may set change in motion by looking for ways to practice being creative in your existing job.

- If you don't like living in the city, and you can't leave right now; try bringing more plants into your home, or consider taking short getaways on the weekends.

- If you don't like your clothes and you don't have the funds to completely replace them all at once; start by buying one new thing that works with what you already own. This way it will feel as though you made two changes toward something new.

- If you think you're not the size you desire, look for ways you can slowly shift your eating habits. This can be a variety of choices; what food you choose to buy, what food you eat, how often you eat, or where you eat.

Practice shifting your perspective whenever you catch yourself not liking a particular aspect of yourself. See how that shift to something you're going toward can change your attitude and feelings about yourself. Then, return to what you wrote here every few days or once a week to remind yourself of the perspectives you decided to adopt. Eventually you'll see a shift in how you're relating to a few of the challenges you feel in your life. This includes a shift in noticing what you're always moving toward, which is liking yourself more.

2. Think of an issue you're struggling with. It can be in your work, in a relationship, something you're trying to do for yourself or another person. Anything.
As you think about it, imagine the best possible outcome for this situation. Take it as far as you can. Then even further and further, as far as you can go.

3. Next, think what the worst possible outcome could be. And take that further and further, as far as you can go.

Really go for it. Don't hold back or judge what comes up. What is the most extreme things you can conceive?

Once you've envisioned both the best and worst outcomes, notice how you feel about each one now — especially the worst one. Have your feelings about either of them changed?

Do this exercise **once a month and monitor how you progress.** Choose a day you'll do it each month.
Mark it in your calendar now!

*"My religion is very simple.
My religion is kindness."*

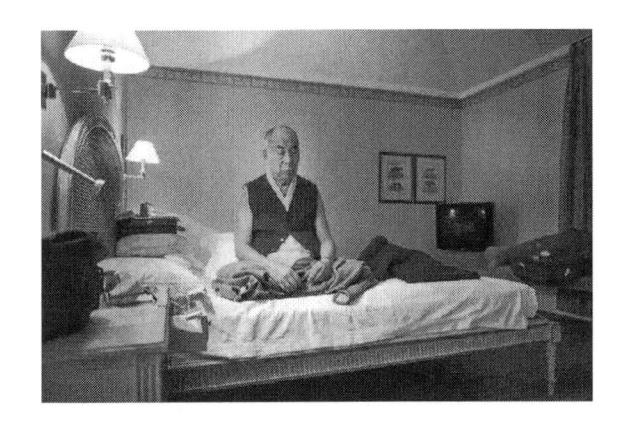

*"This is my simple religion.
There is no need for temples;
no need for complicated philosophy.
Our own brain, our own heart is our temple;
the philosophy is kindness."*

~ Dalai Lama

CHAPTER TWELVE

Spirituality and Kindness

Writing about spirituality can be challenging. I imagine when some of you read the word "spiritual" you smile and relax a little. Others may see it and think, "Oh-no!"

I'm not a spiritual teacher, yet, over time I've come to consider myself a spiritual person.

How about you? Do you consider yourself a spiritual person? I'm not saying you have to be.

The question is for you, as it gives a perspective on how you view the world.

Being a spiritual person was not how I thought of myself for a very long time. As a young man I was completely puzzled by what it meant to be spiritual. In the past, I joked that since I grew up in New York City, I had a mistrust of spirituality (my apologies New York).

I was fairly well-versed on different spiritual traditions; I knew spirituality was not exactly the same as religion, though in some cases it might be. Over the years I met quite a few people who considered themselves spiritual, and most of them maintained a spiritual practice; they chanted, they meditated, or they went to church regularly. What's interesting is that I didn't perceive them as being spiritual. They could breathe deeply, meditate and chant, yet, to me, they were missing an undefinable component.

I'm sure this attributed to my distrust of spirituality, and in return, the concept of what spirituality was or meant eluded me.

In the early 1990's. I was up for a job teaching in the PhD program at the Institute for Transpersonal Psychology, now Sofia University, in Palo Alto, California. During the interview process, the school asked one of my referees on my list who wrote a recommendation for me if I had a spiritual practice. My referee told them I did, and that I meditated.

I protested when he shared this.

"I do not have a spiritual practice!" I said, "I meditate to see if I can sustain my attention for longer periods of time." My protest was truthful. I meditated for precisely this reason and had for many years. While I thought meditating was of great benefit to me, I never felt it gave me a greater understanding around spirituality as a result.

One evening sometime later, the topic of spirituality came up at a dinner party. In that discussion, I thought for the first time that I indeed had an idea what it meant to be spiritual. For me, it was about being kind to both others and myself. I'm not sure what gave me this insight, or where exactly it came from. Yet, I knew I understood it to be true.

I later learned the Dalai Lama held a similar principle about what spirituality is. I shared his quote on this at the beginning of this chapter. "My religion is kindness," he said. This was a new concept to me when I heard it the first time, yet, the instant I heard it; I felt Yeah! that's it! I'm not sure if it makes the same sense to you, or if you have a similar dilemma as I had in not understanding the relationship between kindness and spirituality. What I do know is — when it clicks, you will know.

When I told people about this book, a few responded with "So, it's about compassion'. They were partially right. Kindness and compassion definitely go hand in hand. My intention here is to illuminate the importance of taking real action to create more kindness. These actions may come out of compassion, or the actions may come from other intentions.

The Dictionary definition of compassion is:

Compassion com·pas·sion [kəm'paSHən]

> *noun*
>
> Sympathetic pity and concern for the sufferings or misfortunes of others.
>
> or
>
> Sympathetic consciousness of others' distress together with a desire to alleviate it.

> Synonyms include: Pity, sympathy, empathy, fellow feeling, care, concern, solicitude, sensitivity, warmth, love, tenderness, mercy, leniency, tolerance, **kindness**, humanity, charity.

In looking at the definitions, compassion requires an awareness or attitude you have toward another. Nothing tells us what compassion looks like in action.

A good question to ask is: Am I compassionate?

In 1989, I heard His Holiness the Dalai Lama give a talk on compassion. It was right after he had won the Nobel Peace Prize. There were hundreds of people in attendance, including a large number of serious Buddhist practitioners. In all honesty, it was difficult to listen to the talk. His translator was good, yet for me, the teachings droned on and on. I had a hard time staying awake. I saw others around me drifting and nodding off, which made me feel a little better.

Still, the experience felt meaningful; I thought I should be paying more attention.

At one point a woman near me received a 'transmission'. Although I clearly saw it was powerful for her; I didn't have clue what a 'transmission' was.

In the passage about transmissions and realization from Wikipedia, I put in bold what I think is the essence of a transmission:

> "There is a long history of oral transmission of teachings in Tibetan Buddhism. Oral transmissions by lineage holders traditionally can take place in small groups or mass gatherings of listeners and may last for seconds (in the case of a mantra, for example) or months (as in the case of a section of the Tibetan Buddhist canon). It is held a transmission can even occur without actually hearing, as in Asanga's visions of Maitreya.

> An emphasis on oral transmission as more important than the printed word derives from the earliest period of Indian Buddhism, when it allowed teachings to be kept from those who should not hear them. **Hearing a teaching (transmission) readies the hearer for realization based on it.** The person from whom one hears the teaching should have heard it as one link in a succession of listeners going back to the original speaker: the Buddha in the case of a sutra or the author in the case of a book. Then the hearing constitutes an authentic lineage of transmission. Authenticity of the oral lineage is a prerequisite for realization, hence the importance of lineages."[2]

I thought that was the end my experience with the Dali Lama and compassion, until three weeks later when something odd happened to me.

I woke on a Monday morning, and per my usual routine, I headed to my work as a Feldenkrais practitioner. I noticed that particular morning I felt depressed, and the depressed feeling persisted throughout the day. I was unable to connect my feelings with anything going on in my life. I also noticed I kept thinking all day about the Dalai Lama with no idea why.

Late in the day I had an awareness, and though I can't say it was a transmission, I knew it was significant. It began with this thought, *You know Alan, you are not as compassionate as you think you are.*

That was a bit of a shock, mainly because it felt true. I'd always considered myself as a compassionate person, and now I was aware I had a *long way to go.*

From that moment on, I saw myself in a different light. I believe I encountered a more accurate assessment of myself, one that gave me a new baseline for acting with compassion that started at a much lower place than I'd previously thought. With this realization, I decided to set an intention to develop my capacity for compassion. This realization felt exceptionally meaningful, because I felt it was key to my understanding of compassion, spirituality and kindness. In a nebulous, yet distinct way, it also felt connected to the Dalai Lama.

When looking at the word spiritual, we can see it has a number of different meanings. Spirituality is used to describe feelings and aspects differentiated from the material world. An example of material world includes the everyday plane of reality on which people live. Spirituality is used in reference to the sacred, including the thoughts and feelings concerned with religious values. It's used in relation to supernatural beings or phenomena. As is evident, spirituality is applied to a wide spectrum of concepts and ideas.

Consider this scenario:

A person who describes himself as a 'spiritual' person one day loses his patience in an unpleasant, outspoken way when someone takes too long at the supermarket checkout.

You may think as I once did, that a person 'acting spiritual' may not be as spiritual as they describe themselves. You may assume that because one meditates, goes to church regularly, or prays to Allah several times a day, this doesn't necessarily qualify them as a spiritual person. My challenge to you is this… I think it does.

I think it does because the qualification is in the practice and it is in the attempt toward being a better person. This includes someone who is crabby and gets angry, and it includes people who are *doing the best they can from where they are with the information and abilities they have*. Looking at it this way, being spiritual is more a direction than a place or a state of being that one arrives at.

Some spiritual practices encourage a removal of oneself from the material world. This can occur in degrees, from daily or weekly retreats all the way to living in a cloister or ashram where worldly distractions are removed. In such a cloistered environment, the opportunity exists to dive more deeply into knowing this aspect of oneself. I think all of these scenarios offer valuable and honorable commitments.

I've met people who reject the material world entirely in their spiritual practice. They may use their spirituality as a reason to remove themselves from the world, to help them avoid it and get away from people. If it helps them get closer to God, find peace, or live their intentions to be kinder and more compassionate; then, it's the right path for them. I'm in no position to judge anyone's choices. At the same time, part of me will always wonder what circumstances may enable them to feel more connected with the world, rather than having to disconnect from it.

The idea of connecting more with the world fits in with my premise regarding action being the kingpin to kindness

Connection, in all its forms

One way to think about the purpose of a spiritual practice is that it can help you learn how to more fully connect with yourself. Most people need quiet time to help them learn how to listen to their inner knowing, and there are people who view/need isolation as important to attain this state. Quiet time can help tease apart the habits and compulsions that drive one's thoughts, feelings, and actions to get to the essential, pure YOU that exists within every person.

Spiritual practice can also help you connect with others. For some, spiritual practice includes a focus on creating community based on shared beliefs. This can help them to feel less alone in the world. There are communities who exist primarily for their members, and in other communities, people come together to benefit the larger, surrounding community.

There are spiritual practices that extend the circle of kindness beyond immediate physical locales. For example, Loving-Kindness Meditation (LKM) is a practice in which you direct compassion and wishes for well-being toward yourself and others, real or imagined. In her book, *Lovingkindness: The Revolutionary Art of Happiness,* meditation teacher and author Sharon Salzburg, writes the following:

> "The Dalai Lama has said, "My religion is kindness." If we all adopted such a stance and embodied it in thought and action, inner and outer peace would be immediate, for in reality they are never not present, only obscured, waiting to be re-discovered. This is the work and the power of lovingkindness, the embrace knows no separation between self, others and events—the

affirmation and honoring of a core goodness within others and within oneself."[3]

Researchers Cendri A. Hutcherson, Emma M. Seppala, and James J. Gross studied the effects of LKM and published their results in an article entitled "Loving-Kindness Meditation Increases Social Connectedness". Their study concluded practicing just a few minutes of loving-kindness meditation (LKM) leads to "...increased feelings of social connection and positivity toward novel individuals..."[4]

To rephrase this idea, when we direct kindness toward others, whether we know them or not, even if it is only in the form of thoughts, we feel more connected to those on the receiving end. LKM helps create a strong, valid sense of connection.

Beyond the sense of connection that you feel with yourself and others, there is a sense of connection with something larger than yourself. This 'something larger' may be what you call a higher power. You may call this higher power God, the Universe, or simply nature.

The sense of connection can be general as well... for example: a person's belief that there is a place that exists where one came from before their human conception and birth, a place they feel and believe they will return to after they die.

Regardless of how you may think of it or what you may call it; when this sense of connection with something larger than yourself is present in your life, it can provide you with a greater sense of perspective. This connection can be called a source of light to help guide you in your life.

All spiritual practices revolve, in one way or another, around connection. Whether it's connection with yourself, with a group or larger community, or with something you feel is bigger than you. The need for connection is fundamental to human wellbeing.

Kindness is an act of connection. Kindness is a way of connecting with yourself and a way of connecting with others. Kindness, in this context of being spiritual, is many things — an attitude, a hope, a desire, a way of acting, an attempt at manifesting something better. Most of all, kindness is ultimately the result of all of these things.

Kindness is the outcome of each one of these things that you do, and this includes the action. This is what will help bring about a kinder world.

In all my years of meditating, questioning and seeking, the things that have given me the greatest sense of spirituality were my intentional acts of kindness. I believe, and have observed, that whether you consider yourself religious or spiritual doesn't make a difference; it is the practice of being kind and your kindness people will notice. When you are kind, others will perceive you as a person who brings more light into the world; which may translate to others as a way of being "spiritual".

This brings us back to the beginning of the book.

Kindness is action… and your thoughts are only as good as your actions

While good intentions are important, the best of intentions are meaningless without acting on them in a positive way. Action makes those intentions solid and real, and creates more kindness.

Whether you look at a spiritual practice or religion as a way of life that guides you and provides your life with meaning, or not; I propose you choose to add the practice of kindness to become your way of life. Choose kindness; there are no rules to meditate, no need to follow a guru, no need to join a religion or spiritual group, and no need to ascribe to a set of beliefs and rules. Simply let yourself be guided to practice kindness toward yourself and others, whenever and however you can.

Step twelve to creating and living in a kinder world… being kinder with yourself and others…

Demonstrating kindness in your everyday life

1. If you have a spiritual practice of any kind, take a moment to consider what it connects you with.

Does it give you a deeper connection with yourself? with something larger? with a community?

Imagine now the possible ways you could demonstrate this greater sense of connection by taking a concrete action. Whatever your spiritual practice, find a way to express it tangibly. For example, if you meditate every day for a deeper connection with yourself, find a way to take an action in the world each day, outside of the time you are meditating, that expresses and demonstrates a deeper connection with yourself. It may be creating the 'quiet' you feel when you meditate, bringing it into more hectic situations; or maybe 'going inside' at different moments throughout your day, as a reminder of the quality of feeling you have when you meditate; or do either of these things when you are in the presence of another, to connect with this way of being when you are around others.

If you attend church every Sunday to renew your connection with spirit, find a way to take concrete action each week that comes out of your connection with spirit. Actions that connect you to your own sense of spirit as well as actions that help you connect with others. Look for different ways to practice acts of kindness as a way of creating more connection in your life, with yourself and with others.

2. If you don't have a spiritual practice, make kindness a primary practice in your way of life. We've explored numerous ways to generate more kindness in your life.

   This time, consider the questions in #1 above from the point of view you are part of something larger than yourself, and kindness is truly your way of life.

   What actions can you take to demonstrate kindness on a regular basis — to truly make it become a practice?

WHEN

"Since when," he asked,
*"Are the first line and last line of any poem
where the poem begins and ends?"*
~ **Seamus Heaney**

SINCE

CHAPTER THIRTEEN

You're the Author — A Guide

The End Wait... It's... The Beginning... Wait... it's... the Middle... Wait... it's... The End... Wait... it's... The Beginning... Wait... it's... the Middle...

You're the Author. This is not a mistake. This is the place in which you become the author of the next chapters about how kindness unfolds in your life. They're yours to write. If I could call this chapter Chapters, 13, 14, 15, 16, 17..., I would. The question from here is how will you write them?

Whether you only read the book, did part or none of the exercises in it, my bet is that your thought process regarding kindness has shifted and probably changed. Congratulations!

Perhaps you faithfully practiced the exercises, and discovered you're developing a new relationship with kindness — even better.

Perhaps you're already imagining how you will be the author of new chapters of kindness in your life and you have started acting toward more kindness in a regular way. This is by far the best.

This part of the book could be called the conclusion. Yet, a conclusion implies an ending, or something finished, and this is actually a beginning. I've written about the importance of perspective so here's one more shift you can make:

What you are doing, including this moment, can be seen as a beginning, a middle or an end. If you pause in any one moment, you can shift your perspective of where you are with anything. Choose to shift what you are thinking, what you are feeling, or what you're doing. For example, you may be at the beginning of this sentence, the middle of the paragraph, or the end of this book. The end of this book may come in the middle of your day, the beginning of fixing lunch, or at the end of a deep thought.

The real evidence of any process is how perspectives, tasks, and moments continually evolve and meld into the next and the next, on and on. It's all a question from which perspective you choose to view it.

What is of utmost importance is that you don't let this book end the kindness journey for you.

Don't file this book away on a bookshelf. Keep it close as a reminder. Put it where you can pick it up at any time... someplace you will see it often, where it's easy to reach and open. This place may be the bathroom, near your bed, in the kitchen, or on your desk.

Glance at it frequently to remind you of the ideas you explored, and more importantly, the actions you can take. Share it with others and have conversations about it.

Go back to your notebook. Review your lists. See what has changed for you overtime.

Renew your commitment.

Time off guidelines

In my Professional Feldenkrais Training Programs, I give my trainees 'Time-Off Guidelines'. These are lists of things to do in between segments when they're not in class. The items on the list aren't requirements. They are there to offer structures to help the trainees organize their learning.

I also include one of these lists in their graduation package as a guide for their continued learning and exploration. I've adapted the graduation list for you below, and it is included it in the appendix. I suggest you copy it and print it out, and then place it on your refrigerator or somewhere in your house where you will see it. Make it your reminder that each and every new day presents you with opportunities to create more kindness.

Remember at the beginning when I told you that you were going to have to do something to truly be more kind? It's Take Action!

Acting with kindness is the secret to *kindness.*

Moving Forward

GUIDELINES FOR CREATING MORE KINDNESS...
FOR YOU... FOR OTHERS... FROM NOW ON...

1. Practice... Practice... Practice... Practice... Practice... What you learned about how kindness works in action

2. Practice... Practice... Practice... Practice... Practice...

3. Continue to learn... to be a student... without fear of letting others know about this.

4. Practice... Practice... Practice... Practice... Practice...

5. Talk to everyone you can about Kindness! Learn about it, and experience it, together.

6. Practice... Practice... Practice... Practice... Practice...

7. When something you're practicing is not working... figure out how to make it work!

8. Practice... Practice... Practice... Practice... Practice...

9. Be willing to try things you've never done before.

10. Practice... Practice... Practice... Practice... Practice...

11. Trust what you *don't* know.

12. Practice... Practice... Practice... Practice... Practice...

13. Learn from what you do know.

14. Practice... Practice... Practice... Practice... Practice...

15. Talk to others when you're confused.

16. Practice... Practice... Practice... Practice... Practice...

17. Enjoy your old and new habits... remember how important they are.

18. Practice... Practice... Practice... Practice... Practice...

19. Reinvent kindness for yourself! Reinvent yourself.

20. Practice... Practice... Practice... Practice... Practice...

21. Be happy to learn from all your failures! Appreciate your failures.

22. Practice... Practice... Practice... Practice... Practice...

23. Always be close to a smile on your face when you're practicing being kind.

24. Practice... Practice... Practice... Practice... Practice...

25. Give up as many times as you have to... and always start again.

26. Practice... Practice... Practice... Practice... Practice...

27. Practice... Practice... Practice... Practice... Practice...

28. Practice... Practice... Practice... Practice... Practice...

29. Practice... Practice... Practice... Practice... Practice...

"Stories don't end," he says. "They just turn into new beginnings."

~ Lindsay Eagar from "Hour of the Bees"

Kindness is often thought of as a place we can arrive at, somewhere in the future. The real place of kindness is always right here, right now…
… *always*.

Are we there yet?...
…No…we're still here…

A Message from the Author

"When I was young, I used to admire intelligent people; as I grow older, I admire kind people."

~ Abraham Joshua Heschel

The times we live in appear to be filled with discord. In your world you may experience it politically, at your work, or in your relationships.

Conflict is rampant in our worlds. How can we change that?

As I finished this book (in the USA), Joe Biden is the President and President Donald Trump has left the office and is cosidering another run. Politics or who one holds allegiance to are not important here. What is important is that although Biden won, almost half of the country voted another way, which demonstrates a significant split in the ideology of the USA. This isn't only true in the USA, though. Many countries are divided by different values, and opinions, and beliefs.

As I observed this political climate and thought on it, I began to wonder if there was a person who could bridge the divide. One person who could speak to both sides who both sides would also listen to. I was unable to think of one person.

Upon further thought, I realized that maybe the political arena is a place that is too fraught with divisiveness to find a common meeting ground. It is also unrealistic to think there can be one person who can bridge a divide this vast.

Then, I had an idea — a council, a group who can bring the opposing sides together. Perhaps, the United Nations held this as one of their initial intentions. Once again, I thought maybe politics isn't the place to look for a global and national coming together.

What about different religions? What if the Pope, the Dalai Lama, a great Imam, a great Rabbi formed a council to help us all navigate the challenges the world faces.

This rumination turned out to be a quite a lesson in my own ignorance. I included a Catholic, a Buddhist, an Islamic and a Jewish representative (sounds like the beginning of a joke), and then discovered the incompleteness of my list. I left out the Eastern Orthodox, The Church of Jesus Christ of Latter-Day Saints, Protestantism, Hinduism, New Thought, Neopaganism, Raëlism, Scientology, Serer, Zoroastrianism, Indigenous religions, and, I am sure, many others.

Without fail, my council of four would soon become the United Nations of religions, another 'too big' body to get things done. This council, the United Nations of religions, would soon become complex, as all religions hold what they call Truths, and these beliefs hold strong commitment.

Obviously in my well-intended idea of bringing people together I entered into a rabbit hole that was leading me into a deeper sense of confusion and impossibilities.

There are councils organized for race relations (i.e.: The African American Black Council, The Council for Hispanic Ministries, The Council for Pacific and Asian American Ministries, The Council on Foreign Relations, The Institute of Race Relations... and others) and the environment (i.e.: The Nature Conservancy, Greenpeace... and others) who operate on the principle of a win-win outcome. The Elders, a group of "independent global leaders working together for peace and human rights", was created from a conversation between Richard Branson and Peter Gabriel when they were discussing how communities look to their elders for help, particularly when it comes to resolving disputes

Still, I had to wonder if there's something... an idea, a value, a belief that could bridge these seemingly unsurmountable gaps that exists in the world today. Something that would be agreeable to us all, and no one would argue against. A common ground where we could all meet as equals and find understanding.

I did find it! **Kindness!** It is not 'the' answer, yet I strongly believe kindness is the starting place.

Kindness is a value that, at least on the surface, is appreciated and respected by most people. What if kindness was the starting place, the foundation, the doorway to our conflicts? What if we agreed to begin from this place to find ways of understanding our differences and perchance, see how alike we are?

This may be too grand an idea. It's unlikely to believe the world is suddenly going to shift towards this direction. There are way too many top-down rewards, money, power, and desire for control, for this kind of foundational change to magically happen.

It has been said by many people, in many ways…*if you want to change the world, you have to begin with yourself.*

Maybe for 'the world' to change it begins with you and me. For us to be kinder, kinder toward ourselves and kinder toward others. Maybe we are what the world needs. Thus, this begs the question… How can we be kinder to others and ourselves?

I hope this book is the grand starting point for you.

APPENDICES

APPENDIX A

The worksheet is downloadable at: www.practicing-kindness.com/worksheet

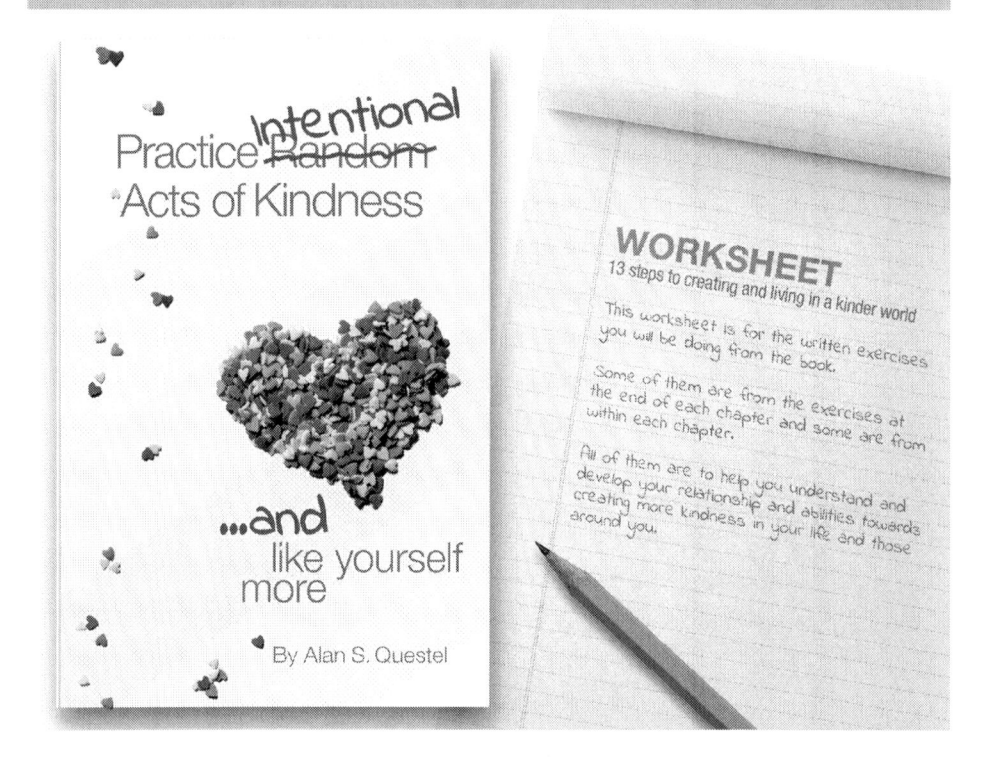

The worksheet is downloadable at: www.practicing-kindness.com/worksheet

Your baseline, or starting place, will provide a frame of reference.
Identify your baseline, and next, set your intentions, and shift your perspective

CHAPTER 1 Cont.

1. Whom are you already kind towards?

Remember, you are kind whether you see it or not, and you are already demonstrating your kindness in many ways. Take a moment to think about it and make a list.

In your answer, include people, animals, plants, insects, groups that you participate in, plus causes and nonprofits you support and you can include yourself on this list. Take your time with your list. Once you feel it's relatively complete, continue to question #2.

As you read Chapter 1 you can add your answers here

CHAPTER 2 Cont.

! Once you have read chapter 2 continue here

Notice the thoughts, feelings, and/or sensations you experience occurring inside of you as you consider each entry on your list..

As you read Chapter 2 you can add your answers here

CHAPTER 3 Cont.

! Once you have read chapter 3 continue here

Go slowly through each entry, pausing with each entry to notice the feelings and sensations that come up in your body.

Notice the distinction between your emotions and the sensations you experience.

As you read Chapter 3 you can add your answers here

CHAPTER 1 Cont.

2. How do you demonstrate this kindness?

Identify the many different ways you demonstrate kindness. For example, how do you let someone know you're feeling kindly towards them? How do you communicate kindness toward an animal, or toward a group or organization? Is it by giving them your attention, taking certain actions, performing tasks or how you speak to them? It's important to list every method of kindness you undertake.
Again, take your time until you feel satisfied with what you wrote.

As you read Chapter 1 you can add your answers here

CHAPTER 2 Cont.

! Once you have read chapter 2 continue here

Notice the thoughts, feelings, and/or sensations you experience occurring inside of you as you consider each entry on your list.

As you read Chapter 2 you can add your answers here

CHAPTER 3 Cont.

! Once you have read chapter 3 continue here

Go slowly through each entry, pausing with each entry to notice the feelings and sensations that come up in your body.

Notice the distinction between your emotions and the sensations you experience.

As you read Chapter 3 you can add your answers here

The worksheet is downloadable at: www.practicing-kindness.com/worksheet

Your Intentions, or what you want to create more of in your life.

CHAPTER 1 Cont.

3. Whom would you like to act kindlier towards?

You're expanding your sense of possibility here. List others you'd like to act kindlier towards; yet, haven't to date.

Again, include any animals, groups and causes, in addition to people. If you didn't include yourself in your answer to the first question, make sure you include yourself now.

Take the time you need to reflect on this list before you go the next one.

As you read Chapter 1 you can add your answers here

CHAPTER 2 Cont.

! Once you have read chapter 2 continue here

Notice the thoughts, feelings, and/or sensations you experience occurring inside of you as you consider each entry on your list.

As you read Chapter 2 you can add your answers here

CHAPTER 3 Cont.

! Once you have read chapter 3 continue here

Go slowly through each entry, pausing with each entry to notice the feelings and sensations that come up in your body.

Notice the distinction between your emotions and the sensations you experience.

As you read Chapter 3 you can add your answers here

CHAPTER 1 Cont.

4. How would you demonstrate kindness towards those on this list?

When you imagine acting kindlier toward those on your list in #3 (Whom do you want to act kindlier towards?), what does that look like? What actions are you willing to take? Be specific with your answers. If possible, include not only the actions you might take, include the frequency and duration of those actions, as well as the places where those actions can take place. In other words, include any details to help you create an explicit vision of what you want to do.

As you read Chapter 1 you can add your answers here

CHAPTER 2 Cont.

! Once you have read chapter 2 continue here

Notice the thoughts, feelings, and/or sensations you experience occurring inside of you as you consider each entry on your list.

As you read Chapter 2 you can add your answers here

CHAPTER 3 Cont.

! Once you have read chapter 3 continue here

Go slowly through each entry, pausing with each entry to notice the feelings and sensations that come up in your body.

Notice the distinction between your emotions and the sensations you experience.

As you read Chapter 3 you can add your answers here

The worksheet is downloadable at: www.practicing-kindness.com/worksheet

Shifting Your Perspective - It's time to think a little differently.

CHAPTER 1

5. Whom can you never imagine acting kindly towards?

Now take the circle of possibility even wider. Are there others to whom you can never in your entire life imagine acting kindly towards? Make a list.

Be brave. Include the names of all the "absolutely not, no way, not a chance in the world" people and organizations you can come up with. Don't worry, you're not going to have to act on this list in any way, unless you choose to. Yet, this list is important. It helps you expand the range of what is actually possible. It may also help give you a sense of perspective when you look back at it later.

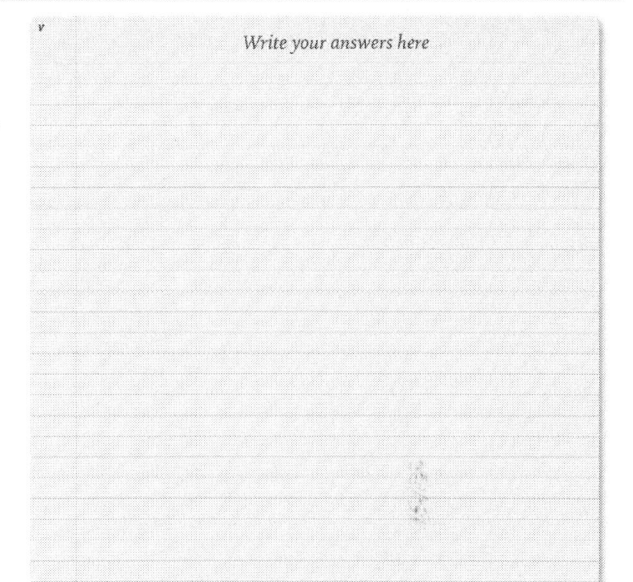

Write your answers here

CHAPTER 1

6. Consider those whom you could never imagine acting kindly towards, and list all the things you can do to act kindly toward them.

Even if this seems impossible, play with it. You may surprise yourself with what you discover.

Write your answers here

The worksheet is downloadable at: www.practicing-kindness.com/worksheet

CHAPTER 2
Complete this sentence:
Kindness is _____
Let yourself go with it.

Don't stop until you've included any and all aspects of kindness you can imagine. Be sure to incorporate all the 'ideals' you have about what kindness is. Consider every aspect of kindness you may be capable of, and all the ways people demonstrate it. Don't read ahead. Finish writing your definition first. Sometimes it helps to let it sit and go back to it over a period of time.

Write your answers here

CHAPTER 3
Writings for Chapter Three Are In The Columns With The Questions From Chapter One - Pages 2-5

Go slowly through each entry, pausing with each entry to notice the feelings and sensations that come up in your body. Notice the DISTINCTIONS between your emotions and the sensations you experience

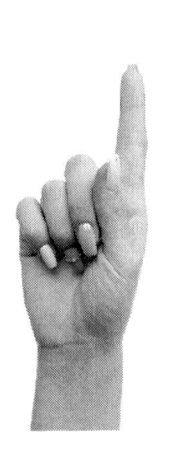

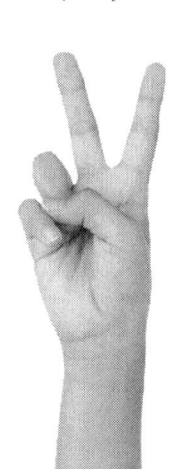

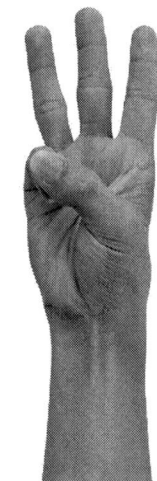

The worksheet is downloadable at: www.practicing-kindness.com/worksheet

CHAPTER 4

Think of a small task you do daily.

Something where your world is uninterrupted and can stay intact, even if you don't do it. I chose brushing my teeth. Maybe for you it's washing the dishes, or turning the lights out when you're not in the room, or hanging your clothes up before you go to bed.

Whatever you choose, make sure the outcome associated with it isn't too big, and there's no time pressure. Keep it small for now.

Choose something you can let develop over time and keep your intention to yourself. This is between you and yourself, keep it secret for now. The reason for this is you're creating a safe learning place where you're the only one evaluating your progress.

When you begin, do it daily. Make it a regular event. Each time you do it, observe what comes up inside you — the conversations you have with yourself, the stories you tell yourself. Most importantly, go easy and be gentle with yourself. Let there be bad days and allow them. Allow good days as well. You'll discover there are great days too, and great days can be just that, great. Each time notice how you feel. Notice you're acting on this no matter how you feel about it.

To be clear here, this is not something you do for just one week and have success. Plan to do it for the next 3 months. This is critical. Because there has to be enough time and space for the ups and downs, and for you to patiently observe what you do as well as what happens inside you.

I recommended that you write down the things you experience.

Writing will help you remain focused and allow you to see patterns in your thoughts, feelings, and actions. You can do this daily, weekly, or at any interval you think works best for you to evaluate.

Write your answers here

---

1. In your perfect world, how would you like others to treat you?

Really go for it, without judgement or second guessing what's possible. Include everything you can imagine. Be generous, be extravagant

2. Choose 3 or 4 people you know and consider what you want to be different in how they treat you.

How will these people act and what will they do to treat you kindlier? Again, let go of judgements and second guessing what they may do or what they are willing to do. You have no idea what someone may or may not do. Be willing to find out.

Taking it a step further from your answers in # 2 (How could the people you know, treat you more kindly?)

For each entry, pause and ask, If they did what I'd like them to do for me, what could I do for them in return, as an act of kindness? What you do in return isn't about it being something big, or even equal to what you want from them. This is about giving. You want to consider little things as well. Write down your answers..

Write your answers here

Write your answers here

Write your answers here

The worksheet is downloadable at: www.practicing-kindness.com/worksheet

CHAPTER 6

Write down the places in your life where you experience pleasure.

Include the small moments, like the first sip of a good cup of coffee or the momentary glance at a beautiful sunset, along with the big moments.

Consider what gives you pleasure on a particular day of the week, and list those.

When you've completed your list — sit with it for a few minutes; then, as you read each entry reflect on how you feel in each of those moments.

See if you can specifically identify the sensations you have in each instance, and where you feel them in your body.

Are they in your face... your chest... several places at once?

Think about how you move when you feel them. Do these sensations differ with different experiences?

Notice how the expression on your face feels. Often our faces subconsciously reveal how we're feeling.

Write your answers here

CHAPTER 7

Look at your day. You may find it filled with five-minute tasks.

Write down all the tasks that involve another person: people at work, if you have children, include them, include your relationships, and include people you encounter when you're out and about. If you have a cat or dog, include the time you spend petting and grooming them.

Pause for a moment and reflect on your list. Are these things you see as five minutes really five minutes? Put a check next to those you truthfully see as five minutes.

Maybe some of your daily tasks require a great deal of your attention and time, while other tasks only a little bit of attention and time. I know when my dog was old, I decided to give him five minutes of my undivided attention every day, and it was hard to do.

Write your answers here

The worksheet is downloadable at: www.practicing-kindness.com/worksheet

CHAPTER 9

1. Where do you think you are generous in your life?

List as many (possible) ways and places, actual and possible, that you can think of. Include the little things, as well as the big things. It's easy to overlook the little ways in which you're generous.

Write your answers here

In each instance, when did it feel like too little, too much, or 'just right'?

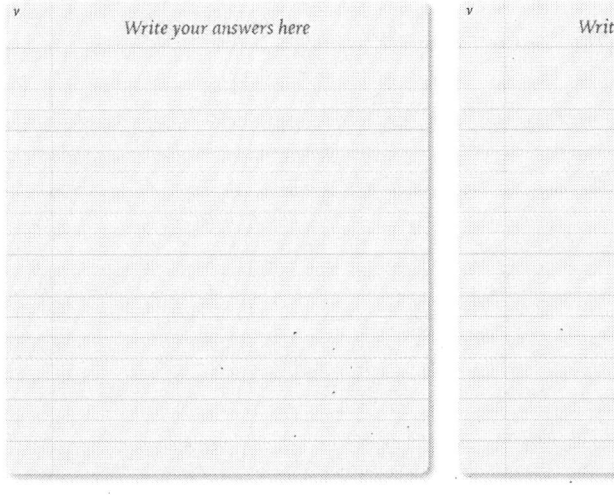

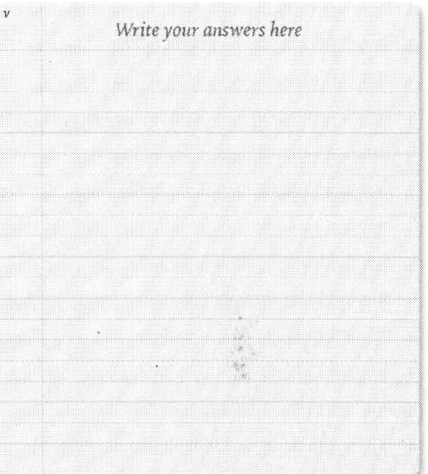

Write your answers here

CHAPTER 9 Cont.

2. Who do you think of as a generous person?

How do they show it?
Does every person on your list do it in the same way?
What are some different ways they show their generosity

Write your answers here

For each person, when do they do it too little, too much or 'just right'?
Or is it the same each time?

Write your answers here

The worksheet is downloadable at: www.practicing-kindness.com/worksheet

CHAPTER 9 Cont.

3. Are there any places in your life where you feel less generous?

Is it toward specific people and/or specific causes or differing events? How do you make those decisions?
What factors do you consider?

Write your answers here

In each of these, what makes it feels like too little?
What would it take to feel 'just right'?

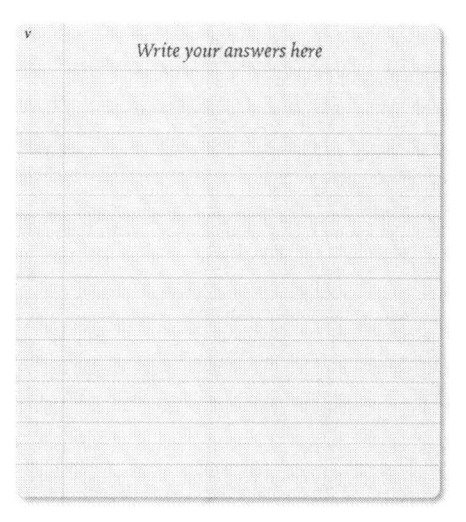

Write your answers here

CHAPTER 9 Cont.

4. Are there places in your life where you felt or feel too generous?

When have you done this?
How do you know it was too generous?

Write your answers here

In each of those places, tell why it felt, or feels, like too much?
What would it take to feel 'just right'?

Write your answers here

The worksheet is downloadable at: www.practicing-kindness.com/worksheet

CHAPTER 9 Cont.

5. Are there people, known to you, whom you do not consider generous?

How do they demonstrate their lack of generosity?
Do they seem ungenerous 100% of the time, or only in certain contexts?

Write your answers here

For each, what do they do that makes it feel like too little?
What would it take to make it feel 'just right'?

Write your answers here

CHAPTER 9 Cont.

6. Are there people you know who are too generous?

For each, what makes it feel like too much?
What are some of the different ways they do this?

Write your answers here

What would it take to make it feel 'just right'?

Write your answers here

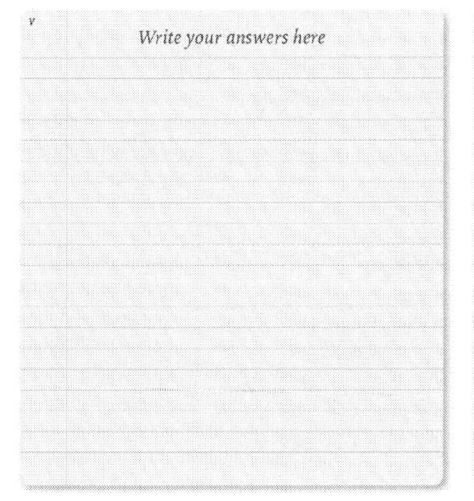

The worksheet is downloadable at: www.practicing-kindness.com/worksheet

Now, answer the questions below with a new focus.

1. Where do you think you are generous in your life?

In any of these places, are you generous so you can get something back? If you are, are there underlying needs you are hoping to get met? What are they? Remember, no judgement. Be kind to yourself.

Write your answers here

2. Who do you think of as a generous person?

When a person gives a gift to you or others, do you interpret their actions as coming from their own needs, rather than a true spirit of generosity? Does it feel as if they want a reciprocal gift when they give? What makes you think that's true?

Write your answers here

CHAPTER 11

1. Make a list of all of the things you want to change in your life.

Take time to look over your list. Notice how many of the things on your list are what you're trying to get away from. Now, rewrite your list from the perspective of what you want to go towards.

For example, if you wrote:
- I want to quit my job.
- I hate living in this city.
- My clothes are all out of style.
- I am too fat... too skinny... too... ???

See how you can turn them into statements that move you toward what you want, similar to these:
- I want to work in a more creative environment.
- I want to live in the country.
- I would love to wear something more stylish.
- I would like to develop healthier eating habits.

Remember, when you shift from 'getting away' to 'going towards', — the change will take time. Most change happens in a series of shifts inside you, a little at a time.

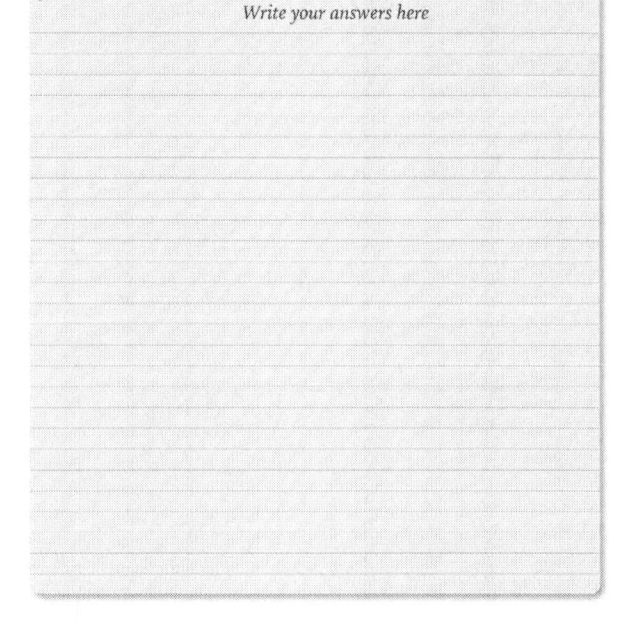

Write your answers here

The worksheet is downloadable at: www.practicing-kindness.com/worksheet

CHAPTER 11 Cont.

A successful strategy may offer these options:

- If you want a more creative job and can't quit your current one right away, you may set change in motion by looking for ways to practice being creative in your existing job.

- If you don't like living in the city, and you can't leave right now; try bringing more plants into your home, or consider taking short getaways on the weekends.

- If you don't like your clothes and you don't have the funds to completely replace them all at once; start by buying one new thing that works with what you already own. This way it will feel as though you made changes toward something new.

- If you think you're not the size you desire, look for ways you can slowly shift your eating habits. This can be a variety of choices; what food you choose to buy, what food you eat, how often you eat, or where you eat.

Practice shifting your perspective whenever you catch yourself not liking a particular aspect of yourself. See how that shift to something you're going toward can change your attitude and feelings about yourself. Then, return to what you wrote here every few days or once a week to remind yourself of the perspectives you decided to adopt. Eventually you'll see a shift in how you're relating to a few of the challenges you feel in your life. This includes a shift in noticing what you're always moving toward, which is liking yourself more.

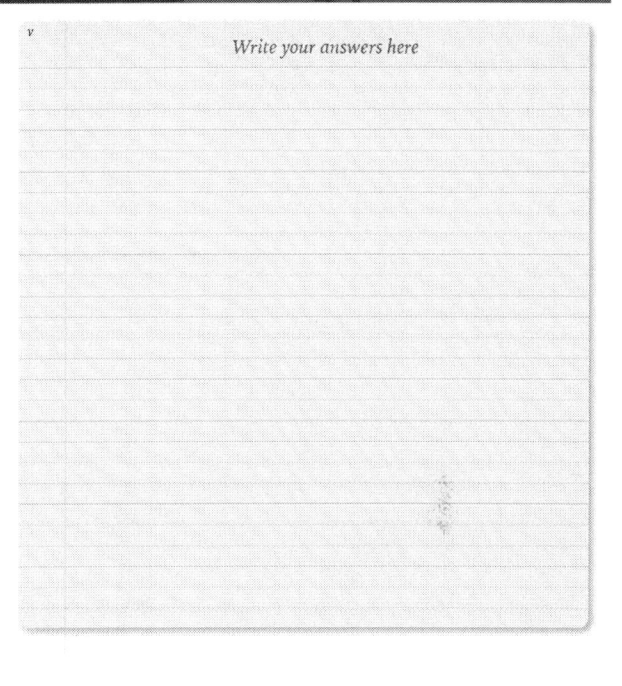

Write your answers here

APPENDIX B

The lists and exercises sorted by chapter

Chapter One Exercises: The Possibility of Kindness — An Exploration

Your first step to creating and living in a kinder world... being kinder with yourself and others...

Identify your baseline, and next, set your intentions, and shift your perspective

Answer the questions in each section. Allow time to explore them. 20-40 minutes is a good start

- Do the best you can with each question, answering as completely as possible. Don't worry if you forget something. You can always come back and add to your answers. Just do not change or erase anything you initially write.

- For now, write your answers to each question on a separate page of its own. You'll look at connecting them later on.

- If you use the worksheet provided at the back of the book and downloadable from my website www.practicing-kindness.com/worksheet, you will see additional columns. Leave them blank, you'll utilize them later.

Your baseline, or starting place, will provide a frame of reference.

1. **Whom are you already kind towards?**
   Remember, you are kind whether you see it or not, and you are already demonstrating your kindness in many ways. Take a moment to think about it and make a list.
   In your answer, include people, animals, plants, insects, groups that you participate in, plus causes and/or nonprofits you support

and you can include yourself on this list.

Take your time with your list. Once you feel it's relatively complete, continue to question #2.

2. ***How do you demonstrate this kindness?***

Identify the many different ways you demonstrate kindness. For example, how do you let someone know you're feeling kindly towards him or her? How do you communicate kindness toward an animal, or toward a group or organization? Is it by giving them your attention, taking certain actions, performing tasks or how you speak to them? It's important to list every method of kindness you undertake.

Again, take your time until you feel satisfied with what you wrote.

Great! Now let's unpack what you wrote, beginning with the first question *Who are you already kind towards?*

How do you feel about what you wrote?

Are you happy with your list?

Did anything about it surprise you? What was it?

Did you leave out a name or two that you would like include? Add them to your list now.

Look at your answers to the second question: How do you demonstrate that kindness? Was it easy or difficult for you to identify all the many ways you show kindness?

Did thinking about this spark even more ideas about how you might demonstrate kindness beyond what you already do?

Did you only consider big acts, or did you include the little things, like holding the door open or saying, "Thank you"?

These lists represent your baseline or starting place and provide a frame of reference. Periodically returning to this reference point will help you evaluate your progress toward developing a new relationship with kindness. This baseline will give you an enhanced perspective over time.

Your *Intentions*, or what you want to create more of in your life.

The next set of questions will help you get clearer.

This may be how you thought you would begin this process, but you needed your baseline first.

3. Whom would you like to act kindlier towards?

You're expanding your sense of possibility here. List others you'd like to act kindlier towards; yet, haven't to date.

Again, include any animals, groups and/or causes, n addition to people. If you didn't include yourself in your answer to the first question, make sure you include yourself now.

Take the time you need to reflect on this list before you go the next one.

4. How would you demonstrate kindness towards those on this list?

When you imagine acting kindlier toward those on your list in #3, what does that look like? What actions are you willing to take?

Be specific with your answers. If possible, include not only the actions you might take, include the frequency and duration of those actions, as well as the places where those actions can take place. In other words, include any details to help you create an explicit vision of what you want to do. For example, you may want to:

Call someone you know. Maybe it's someone who is going through a difficult time, or someone with whom you haven't spoken to in a while. It may be someone you know who wants to hear from you.

For no reason except to be kind, offer to do a chore for a friend.

Help them fold the laundry, or drive them somewhere, or run an errand. Anything that may help them out.

Brush your cat or dog regularly, once a week.

Volunteer at your church, mosque or place of worship, at a food kitchen, or at your favorite charity.

When you're finished, pause and consider whether there is anything else you can add.

Now, let's look at your answers.

When you considered the question 3 (Whom do you want to act kindlier towards?), did anyone come immediately to mind?

If so, was that person already on your first list?

Was it someone you want to act even more kindly towards? Or did you only think of people you have yet to act kindly towards?

Did a new relationship or an older one come to mind?

Regarding question 4 (How would you demonstrate this kindness?), was it hard to come up with ways to show kindness? Are you willing to take the chance to say how you really want to act?

These second two lists express your Intentions, what you want to create more of in your life. Intentions are an important part of this process; they are not the same as goals. Goals are things achieved in the future. Intentions remind us how we desire to live our lives in each and every moment.

My intention is to help you create the kindness you desire in your life, and for you to find more of the connection you're looking for with yourself and others. Another intention I have for this process is helping you discover many more and different ways to create ongoing kindness in the world beyond yourself. As I mentioned previously, this is a kindness journey, a continuing process of self-development, it's not a final resting place.

Take a moment to go over all four lists and add anything you feel moved to add. As you do so, resist changing or crossing anything out. Your first impulses often reveal your true feelings and are valuable. Please remember, there's no judgement here. These exercises are designed for gaining awareness and setting intentions.

Shifting Your Perspective

It's time to think a little differently.

5. *Whom can you <u>never</u> imagine acting kindly towards?*

Now take the circle of possibility even wider. Are there others to whom you can never in your entire life imagine acting kindly towards? Make a list.

Be brave. Include the names of all the "absolutely not, no way, not a chance in the world" people and organizations you can come up with. Don't worry, you're not going to have to act on this list in any way, unless you choose to. Yet, this list is important. It helps you expand the range of what is actually possible. It may also help give you a sense of perspective when you look back at it later.

Let's reflect a bit

Look at your answers to questions #1 (Whom are you already kind towards?) and question #3 (Whom would you like to act kindlier towards?).

Are the two lists about the same length? Or is one much longer than the other?

Did you include yourself on both lists, or on only one… or neither?

It's important and interesting how we can interpret the lengths of each list. If you have more answers on question #1 (Whom are already kind towards?), then it's possible developing more kindness is necessary in only a few areas. Perhaps, another way to think about it is this short list represents the hardest ones to act kindly towards. What some may perceive as a 'short list' could actually be a 'hard list.'

If your list in question #3 (Whom would you like to act kindlier towards?) is longer, you might imagine that you have a lot of work to do, and you might think it's going to be hard going. Or it could simply be a reflection of how much kindness you want to demonstrate and create around you.

Most likely you fall somewhere between all these interpretations: of wanting a wider range of kindness, and/or accepting there may be difficult challenges thrown in. Either way, as you progress you will gain new perspectives through different ideas and actions. With progressive steps, you will find your responses start to shift and change.

The length of each list isn't important. Seeing them in relation to each other is to give you an idea of your kindness landscape, to see the range of kindness presently existing in your life and the degree of desire you have, or want to have, to create greater kindness around you.

Remember… Your desire to have more kindness in your life is likely the reason you bought this book. *This desire is itself evidence of your capacity to create more kindness in your life.*

Question #2 (How do you demonstrate this kindness?) and question *#4 (How would you demonstrate this kindness?)* are the same, but with a twist. One is answered in terms of what you already do, and the other in terms of what you may do.

Consider:
- How do your answers compare? How different or similar are they?
- Do you wish some of the behaviors on one list were possible on the other?
- Are there things on one list that are absolutely unimaginable on the other?
- Do you act differently when it's for real than when you are imagining kindness?

These two lists can reveal a great deal about you. For one, they reflect how you value kindness. And second, the differences between what you already do (your baseline) and what you would like to do (your intentions) help you recognize where you're starting from and the direction you're heading in.

Now look at question #5 *(Whom can you never imagine acting kindly towards?)*.

This question can help you gain some perspective on what is truly possible for you as your endeavor to cultivate more kindness.

It's likely the answers you gave in question #3 (Whom would you like to act kindlier towards?), already presents a certain level of challenge for you. If they were not challenging, you may already be acting kindlier in their direction. In either case then, considering kindness to those on your list in question #5 (Whom could you never imagine acting kindly towards?) may seem impossible — even as a fantasy it's not even up for consideration!

Yet, despite seemingly daunting, look over your list of those you could never imagine acting kindly towards. Take some time to dwell on each as if you truly considered acting kindlier towards them. How might you go about it? (Remember, this is only an exercise, you don't have to actually do it).

We are ready for the last question:

6. Consider those whom could you <u>never</u> imagine acting kindly towards, and list all the things you can do to act kindly toward them.

Even if this seems impossible, play with it. You may surprise yourself with what you discover.

Our perspective determines how we see things. It precedes experience and influences the way we view and understand the world.

Later on, we'll look more deeply at this idea. For now, I invite you to do a little experiment.

7. Look over all your lists once more but do it in reverse order.

Begin with lists #5 and #6—the lists of those whom you could never act kindly towards, how you can do it and what it will take to actually do it, still imagined.

As you read, reflect on each person, animal, group, etc. on your list. Imagine what it will look like. Include as many details as you can imagine: the actual things you can do, how it would feel, what words you may use.

It's important to take your time. Don't go too quickly.

Look at your answers to questions #3 and #4, the lists of those whom you would like to act kindlier towards and how you may go about that. Again, take your time. Thoughtfully consider everyone on your list and the actions you can take towards them,

What happened when you read your lists in this reverse order?

Did it get any easier to see yourself actually acting kindlier toward those whom, till now, you had only thought about acting kindly towards (list #3)?

Did something shift when you considered those you thought you could never act kindly towards? Does the feeling of challenge diminish? What about your sense of possibility? Did you feel it begin to expand?

Can you begin to imagine yourself having a greater capacity for kindness than you previously thought possible?

This part of the process is meant to show you what might have previously seemed beyond your reach may actually be closer than you think. This isn't about giving you the means for doing it, it's about planting the possibility in your consciousness.

As a reminder, the lists you created comprise your baseline and intentions; these will provide you with a reference point to help you gauge your progress on this journey of cultivating more kindness.

In the following chapters, you'll have the chance to reflect more on these initial lists, add to them, and move things over from your imagined list to one of things you're already doing.

I am on this journey with you. You are off to a great start!

Chapter Two Exercises: Turning Kindness into a Verb

We've discussed the first step to creating and living in a kinder world...
being kinder with yourself and others... here is your second step
Identifying your thoughts and feelings

At this point you will learn how to identify your thoughts, feelings and sensations, and distinguish them from each other to see how they influence your responses and reactions. This is your potential to be empowered. Distinguishing of your thoughts, feelings and sensations can lead you further into self-awareness, with enhanced self-awareness, you're able to act intentionally, this will take you closer to fulfilling your desire and stated intention of acting kindlier toward others and yourself.

Go now to the lists you made earlier in Chapter One for Baseline (questions #1 and #2) and Intentions (questions #3 and #4)

Start with Question #1, and notice the thoughts, feelings, and/or sensations you experience occur inside as you consider each entry on your list.

There's no rush. Sometimes it's hard to identify what exactly you are experiencing, and it takes a few minutes. Start with your body. That's often easiest to identify.

Write down your observations.

The worksheet in the appendix is set up for you to do this with the questions from each question.

Do this with the answers from each question.

What you write may not make a lot of sense right now. So, if there's a place where you seem tunable to name what you think, feel or sense, put a star next to it as a reminder to go back and reflect on it later.

Remember, this is just the beginning. You are practicing how to identify with these aspects of yourself. There's no right way or wrong way to do it. You're already on your way to awareness and success to being more kind simply by having the willingness to begin and do it.

Chapter Three Exercises: What Others Think... Feelings of Kindness...and more...

The third step to creating and living in a kinder world... being kinder with yourself and others...

Exploring the distinctions of kindness

Our next step in understanding these concepts comes with exploring these distinctions through the six lists you created in Chapter One.

As you move forward, I encourage you to make a note about what you're experiencing whenever you hit a spot that feels difficult or challenging. These moments will be important to refer to as you move forward.

What we're doing is building on each thing you do. The first part of this clarity process was in Chapter Two, page 49. I strongly suggest you now do it again, because you'll most likely find your responses have changed or seem clearer. Think of it as getting to know yourself better and having more choices in your life. Once this is completed, go to the next steps listed below.

1. Pull out and review your first two lists from Chapter One: *Who you're already kind towards and How you demonstrate kindness.* Go slowly through each entry, pausing with each entry to notice the feelings and sensations that come up in your body. Notice the distinction between your emotions and the sensations you experience.

   Since these lists include those you already feel and act kindly towards, it may be easier to separate out your feelings from your sensations. If it's not easy, remember you aren't expected to be good at this. Simply asking the question will help you gain understanding.

2. When you're done with the first two lists, turn to the third list in Chapter One *(Who you would like to act kindlier towards)* and do the same thing, pausing with each entry to notice your feelings and
sensations. Notice if there are differences in your feelings and sensations than when you read the first two lists.

3. Follow the identical process for the fourth list *(How you demonstrate kindness)*. Again, go slowly, and observe what feelings and sensations you can identify. Notice if different feelings arise when you think of actually doing something rather than just thinking about it?

4. Repeat the process with your fifth list *(Who could you never imagine acting kindly towards)* What feelings and sensations come up here? Are they stronger than in the previous lists? Is it harder to tolerate? Are you able to find the feelings and sensations?

Good work! **Take a short break and come back when you're ready to begin Part Two of this exercise.**

When you started, I asked you to make a note of all the places you felt difficulty or challenged while reviewing your lists. Choose one of those places and consider if you can reverse this feeling in the way discussed earlier — If I feel this way (angry, sad, frustrated,) can I change the way I feel?

Take your time with it. See if you feel something start to shift, can you identify if it's feelings or sensations.

When you're ready, proceed to the next difficult or challenging place/person and do the same thing. You'll perform this process with each person/place you felt was difficult or challenging.

Some situations may feel easy to shift while others may feel impossible. Right? Be kind to yourself. There's no right or wrong here. You're simply practicing how to notice your feelings and sensations, and what may provoke them.

Your final step is to go through your lists one more time, and when you get to a difficult place, imagine staying with your feelings and acting in a different way - as a conscious response versus a natural reaction. For example, if you feel angry toward a person, can you imagine cooking a meal for them? Or if someone hurt your feelings and you withdrew from them, can you imagine the two of you having a conversation about their day or your day?

What's it like to hold two seemingly disparate or opposite things? Can you describe it?

You won't always be able to imagine doing these things with the feeling you have, yet, you may surprise yourself. You may discover that through imagining that you chose to act differently, your feelings start to change. You may discover, several will take less energy to change than you thought, and many may seem more possible than you thought!

Thinking, feeling, and sensing the world you inhabit includes acting in it. Amazingly, it's all continually occurring within you at the same time. When you change one thing about yourself, the others will start to change, too.

Chapter Four Exercises: What's So Hard?

The fourth step to creating and living in a kinder world... being kinder with yourself and others...

Doing one thing well

Think of a small task you do daily. Something where your world is uninterrupted and can stay intact, even if you don't do it. I chose brushing my teeth. Maybe for you it's washing the dishes, or turning the lights out when you're not in the room, or hanging your clothes up before you go to bed.

Whatever you choose, make sure the outcome associated with it isn't too big, and there's no time pressure. Keep it small for now.

Choose something you can let develop over time and keep your intention to yourself. This is between you and yourself, keep it secret for now. The reason for this is you're creating a safe learning place where you're the only one evaluating your progress.

When you begin, do it daily. Make it a regular event. Each time you do it, observe what comes up inside you – –the conversations you have with yourself, the stories you tell yourself. Most importantly, go easy and be gentle with yourself. Let there be bad days and allow them. Allow good days as well. You'll discover there are great days too, and great days can be just that, great. Each time notice how you feel. Notice you're acting on this no matter how you feel about it.

To be clear here, this is not something you do for just one week and have success. Plan to do it for the **next 3 months.** This is critical. Because there has to be enough time and space for the ups and downs, and for you to patiently observe what you do as well as what happens inside you.

I recommended that you write down the things you experience.

Writing will help you remain focused and allow you to see patterns in your thoughts, feelings, and actions. You can do this daily, weekly, or at any interval you think works best for you to evaluate.

Good luck! Remember, change takes time.

Chapter Five Exercises: Self-Kindness

The fifth step to creating and living in a kinder world... being kinder with yourself and others...

Treating yourself a little bit better and mantras

Simple action steps:

1. From your lists, identify something you would like someone else to do for you, and do it for yourself. Do it with the intention of being kinder to yourself because you want to be kind to yourself and you deserve it. Not because it's in reaction to you not getting something.

2. From the list you generated in response to the question How could the people you know treat you more kindly? select one person (more if you like) and identify ways you can act kindlier towards them, without them changing how they are towards you first.

3. Use your mantras— Is this a good time to be thinking about this? I am driving around in a bad neighborhood, I need to get out of here. This is a dead end. — when you find yourself doing or thinking about something when it's not the right place or time, and when your thoughts are running in loops. Practice interrupting yourself with the mantra in the middle of the behavior until it becomes a habit. You decide which ones work best in which moments.

4. When you find you're having unkind thoughts about yourself, such as "I'm not good enough," "I'll never learn this," or "Everyone's better at this than I am," add onto each thought, "And I'm doing the best I can." It's unlikely you'll get rid of these thought right away, adding that last reassurance you're okay will give you a better chance at moving forward.

I am not good enough.

And...I am doing the best I can!

Is this a good time to be thinking about this?

No.

I'm driving around in a bad neighborhood.

I need to get out of here.

I'm at a dead end.

Time to move on.

Chapter Six Exercises: It's All in How You Move

The sixth step to creating and living in a kinder world... being kinder with yourself and others...

Getting comfortable and moving in ways that 'you like the way' it feels

Now it's time to explore how you find pleasure in simply moving.

Get out your notebook

Write down the places in your life where you experience pleasure. Include the small moments, like the first sip of a good cup of coffee or the momentary glance at a beautiful sunset, along with the big moments.

Consider what gives you pleasure on a particular day of the week, and list those.

When you've completed your list — sit with it for a few minutes; then, as you read each entry reflect on how you feel in each of those moments.

See if you can specifically identify the sensations you have in each instance, and where you feel them in your body.

Are they in your face... your chest... several places at once?

Think about how you move when you feel them.

Do these sensations differ with different experiences?

Notice how the expression on your face feels. Often our faces subconsciously reveal how we're feeling.

These sensations will be part of what you look for in the next exercises. You have a choice to do either 1, 2 or 3, or all of them. Do whichever works best for you.

1. **Look for moments in your day where you can explore the quality of how you feel when you move.** Pick simple tasks. Ones you do frequently throughout the day are great; getting in and out of bed, cleaning the house, or getting dressed are a few examples.

    While doing each task, slow your movements down just a little and find a way to move that you like the way it feels.

    Feel each part of your body and notice if you smiling or thinking it feels good? That will tell you when you're there. Let yourself feel good doing it.

    Interchange the tasks you focus on throughout your week or month if that makes it more interesting or fun.

2. Set an alarm to go off every hour, or every two or three hours… you decide. This can be on your phone; use what is convenient. When your alarm goes off, continue what you're doing and change it around to a focus on moving in a way that you like the way it feels. For example, sitting at the computer where you don't move much, take the moment to get a little more comfortable in your chair, or perhaps adjust the screen and place your feet in a different position. If you aren't able to do this when the alarm goes off, let it go and wait for the next alarm.

3. Throughout the day, pause and consider if you feel comfortable. If you do, make a small adjustment to get more comfortable, move to where you feel good. If you don't feel comfortable, see what small adjustment you can do so you are. Do this throughout your entire day whenever you think about it.

Continue expanding on it from this moment on until it feels as though it is second nature, and you don't need to remind yourself because it happens spontaneously.

Chapter Seven Exercises: Kindness... 5 minutes a day...

The seventh step to creating and living in a kinder world... being kinder with yourself and others...

Five minutes a day

Now let's explore this concept of devoting FIVE minutes a day to an act of kindness. This is the most important process in the book; over time it can and will significantly shift your relationship with kindness. Please take the time needed to consider and practice this exercise; if now is not the right time to dive in, find time to come back and do it later.

You want to always appreciate what you can do and acknowledge your readiness when it's the right time.

If you fall down in the process and don't do what you intend, pick yourself up and begin again. It's that simple.

This exercise is about taking action. As you learned, your feelings may feel incongruent as you perform the task you chose to do each day; there may be a difference in how you feel before you do the task and the moment you do the task. Do it, and take action, anyway.

It will be easier to work with a person on your list with whom you're already acting kindly toward. It's also fine if you choose to work with another person on your list.

Spend five minutes a day directing your attention toward this person.

You can approach this in various ways. You can spend five minutes a day thinking about this person, wondering how they are or what they may be doing. Better yet, spend five minutes doing something you consider kind with or for them; talk with them on the phone, write them an e-mail, or sit quietly with them.

Do your five minutes all at one time, if possible. If not, do a few moments at a time throughout the day. Just do it, five minutes every day!

I recommend reminding yourself of your intention first thing in the morning when you wake; and again, before you sleep at night, take a few moments to reflect on your intention. I advise this because your life can get busy and remembering to do this is harder than you may imagine. It will help immeasurably to put a reminder note near your bed, on the refrigerator, or at your desk. If you discover you completely forgot, be kind with yourself. There's always the next day.

As you read on, you'll find innumerable, perhaps unexpected, ways to include the person you chose in your thoughts and actions. For now, choose how you want to spend your five minutes expressing more kindness.

Chapter Eight Exercises: Look... and listen

The eighth step to creating and living in a kinder world... being kinder with yourself and others...

Listening and intentional chit chat

In this section, you'll practice two things you can do to promote kindness, both involving momentary acknowledgment of another person.

To introverts who may consider these actions beyond their tolerance level; you don't have to do what I suggest here. There are a variety of ways you can generate more kindness. Be kind to yourself if this task feels too hard right now.

This goes for everyone. You can always choose when you want to do it. Remember, do this practice when you feel safe or ready, even if it's only once a day or once a week.

One of the safest places to experiment with full presence in listening is on the phone when you're speaking to a stranger from an airline, the phone company or a customer service help line.

Begin by asking the person on the other end of the line how they're doing that day. I do this frequently, and the most common response I hear is surprise in their voice as they thank me for asking. You may not be surprised to learn the conversations usually take an easier trajectory when they begin this act of kindness.

Here's your kindness task:

1. Throughout your day, whenever you find yourself in an interaction with a stranger, pause for a moment and ask them how they are. Give them your complete attention for a few moments. (Remember, you can practice this on the phone if it's easier).

Observe how they respond. Do they brighten up a bit? Do they sound and feel a bit more human to you? How do you feel as you walk away (or hang up)? Did that little act of kindness appear to help both of you feel a little better?

2. The next time you run into a person in your life who usually over-demands your attention, take a deep breath, slow yourself down, and settle in to listen to them. Ask them questions as you listen, this can be short time span, a few minutes. It's okay at a certain point to look at your watch and say, "My apologies. I have to go now. It was nice chatting with you."

You will definitely see results from this over time. You will significantly increase the balance in your kindness account!

Chapter Nine Exercises: The Twins — Generosity and Kindness...

The ninth step to creating and living in a kinder world... being kinder with yourself and others...

Being generous... to yourself and to others

1. **Practicing being generous by giving just a little bit more.**

    If you've ever had a job where your earnings were from tips, this will definitely resonate with you. Tip just a little bit more. A few places and ways it's easy to practice this are: after a meal in a restaurant, when you get you haircut, or when you take a taxi, Uber, or Lyft.

    For example, for every five dollars (or less) of a tip, add one dollar more. If your calculation says the tip is $3, give $4. If $10, give $12. If the tip comes to $20, give $24. I want to stress these amounts are a suggestion; only do it only if it's affordable to you. In any case, it's not the percentage or the amount that's important, it's that you are being intentionally more generous with giving. You're doing it with the motivation that you'll receive nothing in return from the person receiving the extra tip.

    Be prepared for challenging internal conversations. I recently took friends to dinner and the bill came to $70.00. I usually tip 20%, which would be $14.00, bringing the total to $84.00. I had $90.00 in my wallet, and I decided to give the whole $90.00. To my surprise, the minute I had the thought to give all I had in my wallet, not just 20%, I had internal conflict. I thought, Is this too much? Should I do it? on and on. I ended up giving the full $90.00. As I left the restaurant the waitress stopped me and said, "You made my night!" Which made my night!

2. **Praise and acknowledgment** - Give a compliment and praise someone when you see them doing something well. Make it a habit.

3. **Practice being kind to yourself** - This next process is open-ended; you decide how you want to do it.

    Each week give yourself something, a gift. It can be extra money or extra time just for yourself. It can be allowing yourself the pleasure of doing one thing you like to do. Use your imagination.

    Whatever you give yourself can change week to week, if you choose to do that.

Quick start ideas...
- put aside $15 to buy yourself something special
- save the $15 over several weeks to get something you've wanted for a while and didn't have the money.
- once a week treat yourself to a massage, a facial, or a shave.
- set aside time to go on a favorite hike or walk.

The important point is to practice this regularly, weekly when possible. Choose something that's affordable in terms of cost and/or time. Whatever you decide to do, make sure you do it!

It is to your immediate benefit to practice being more generous to yourself and to develop the practice until it becomes a habit.

In the exercises above you're practicing being kind to others and yourself in small, regular ways over a period of time that will add up to measurable shifts in how you give and receive.

4. **Do something kind for a someone you don't know directly.**

    You can do this in a multitude of ways. You may decide to donate to a cause or a non-profit. It can be a one-time donation or a recurring weekly or monthly donation. This can be a small amount; every dollar donation adds up, don't reject the amount as too small!

Alternatively, you may give your spare change to a person on the street asking for help. I recently had a credit in a store where I don't usually shop. I chose something in the store for myself, and I still had $15 left. I wandered around looking for a way to spend that remaining $15 credit without any luck at finding or thinking of anything I wanted or needed. I approached a young person looking at jackets and gave the credit to him. I wish I had a picture of the smile on his face. Perhaps you can imagine the smile on my face, as well!

Chapter Ten Exercises: Tough Love, A Good Thing

The Tenth Step to creating and living in a kinder world... being kinder with yourself and others...

Conversations

1. Think of someone you believe would appreciate an honest conversation with you, and benefit from it. Choose someone you feel comfortable approaching to give feedback and suggestions on how they might improve and better themselves. It's important how you do this, as it can be tricky.

2. Start by looking for a moment where they express a need or deep desire to understand or change something about themselves. Then ask them if they are interested or if it's okay to give them feedback. As I said, this can be sensitive. You don't want to put them off, if they aren't open or ready, let it go. Practice doing this in your imagination, which will shift something in how you understand and interact with them.
   AND, there may be another opportunity later when they are open to it. Just remember, it's always important how you begin the

conversation. Keep reminding yourself you are doing this as an act of kindness to yourself and also to them.

3. Identify a 'conversation' you repeatedly have with yourself that loops over and over through your mind. It can be an event or another person. Decide what you want to do about it.

Can you let it go? or is it something that needs to be dealt with? If you decide it needs to be dealt with, make the time to approach the person for a conversation, even if it feels challenging. **Be willing to find out if it can be resolved.**

Remind yourself you're doing this as an act of kindness to yourself and to them.

Chapter Eleven Exercises: Change Your Perspective, Change Your Life

Kindness Depends on How You See Things

Step eleven to creating and living in a kinder world... being kinder with yourself and others...

Going toward something and shifting your perspective

1. Make a list of all of the things you want to change in your life. Take time to look over your list.

Notice how many of the things on your list are what you're trying to get away from. Now, rewrite your list from the perspective of what you want to go towards.

For example, if you wrote:
- *I want to quit my job.*
- *I hate living in this city.*
- *My clothes are all out of style.*

- *I am too fat… too skinny… too… ???*

See how you can turn them into statements that move you toward what you want, similar to these:
- *I want to work in a more creative environment.*
- *I want to live in the country.*
- *I would love to wear something more stylish.*
- *I would like to develop healthier eating habits.*

Remember, when you shift from 'getting away' to 'going towards', — the change will take time. Most change happens in a series of shifts inside you, a little at a time.

A successful strategy may offer these options:

- If you want a more creative job and can't quit your current one right away, you may set change in motion by looking for ways to practice being creative in your existing job.

- If you don't like living in the city, and you can't leave right now; try bringing more plants into your home, or consider taking short getaways on the weekends.

- If you don't like your clothes and you don't have the funds to completely replace them all at once; start by buying one new thing that works with what you already own. This way it will feel as though you made two changes toward something new.

- If you think you're not the size you desire, look for ways you can slowly shift your eating habits. This can be a variety of choices; what food you choose to buy, what food you eat, how often you eat, or where you eat.

Practice shifting your perspective whenever you catch yourself not liking a particular aspect of yourself. See how that shift to something you're going toward can change your attitude and feelings about yourself. Then, return to what you wrote here every few days or once a week to remind yourself of the perspectives you decided to adopt. Eventually you'll see a shift in how you're relating to a few of the challenges you feel in your life. This includes a shift in noticing what you're always moving toward, which is liking yourself more.

1. Think of an issue you're struggling with. It can be in your work, in a relationship, something you're trying to do for yourself or another person. Anything.
    As you think about it, imagine the best possible outcome for this situation. Take it as far as you can. Then even further and further, as far as you can go.

2. Next, think what the worst possible outcome could be. And take that further and further, as far as you can go.

Really go for it. Don't hold back or judge what comes up. What is the most extreme things you can conceive?

Once you've envisioned both the best and worst outcomes, notice how you feel about each one now — especially the worst one. Have your feelings about either of them changed?

Do this exercise **once a month and monitor how you progress.**
Choose a day you'll do it each month.
Mark it in your calendar now!

Chapter Twelve Exercises: Spirituality and Kindness

Step twelve to creating and living in a kinder world... being kinder with yourself and others...

Demonstrating kindness in your everyday life

If you have a spiritual practice of any kind, take a moment to consider what it connects you with.

Does it give you a deeper connection with yourself? with something larger? with a community?

Imagine now the possible ways you could demonstrate this greater sense of connection by taking a concrete action.

Whatever your spiritual practice, find a way to express it tangibly. For example, if you meditate every day for a deeper connection with yourself, find a way to take an action in the world each day, outside of the time you are meditating, that expresses and demonstrates a deeper connection with yourself. It may be creating the 'quiet' you feel when you meditate, bringing it into more hectic situations; or maybe 'going inside' at different moments throughout your day, as a reminder of the quality of feeling you have when you meditate; or do either of these things when you are in the presence of another, to connect with this way of being when you are around others.

If you attend church every Sunday to renew your connection with spirit, find a way to take concrete action each week that comes out of your connection with spirit. Actions that connect you to your own sense of spirit as well as actions that help you connect with others.

Look for different ways to practice acts of kindness as a way of creating more connection in your life, with yourself and with others.

If you don't have a spiritual practice, make kindness a primary practice in your way of life. We've explored numerous ways to generate more kindness in your life.

This time, consider the questions in #1 above from the point of view you are part of something larger than yourself, and kindness is truly your way of life.

What actions can you take to demonstrate kindness on a regular basis — to truly make it become a practice?

Chapter Thirteen Exercises

You're the Author — A Guide
The End...Wait... It's... The Beginning... Wait... it's... the Middle... Wait it's... The End...... Wait... it's... The Beginning... Wait... it's... the Middle...

Moving Forward

GUIDELINES FOR CREATING MORE KINDNESS... FOR YOU... FOR OTHERS... FROM NOW ON...

1. Practice... Practice... Practice... Practice... Practice... What you learned about how kindness works in action

2. Practice... Practice... Practice... Practice... Practice...

3. Continue to learn... to be a student... without fear of letting others know about this.

4. Practice... Practice... Practice... Practice... Practice...

5. Talk to everyone you can about Kindness! Learn about it, and experience it, together.

6. Practice... Practice... Practice... Practice... Practice...

7. When something you're practicing is not working... figure out how to make it work!

8. Practice... Practice... Practice... Practice... Practice...

9. Be willing to try things you've never done before.

10. Practice... Practice... Practice... Practice... Practice...

11. Trust what you don't know.

12. **Practice... Practice... Practice... Practice... Practice...**

13. **Learn from what you do know.**

14. **Practice... Practice... Practice... Practice... Practice...**

15. **Talk to others when you're confused.**

16. **Practice... Practice... Practice... Practice... Practice...**

17. **Enjoy your old and new habits... remember how important they are.**

18. **Practice... Practice... Practice... Practice... Practice...**

19. **Reinvent kindness for yourself! Reinvent yourself.**

20. **Practice... Practice... Practice... Practice... Practice...**

21. **Be happy to learn from all your failures! Appreciate your failures.**

22. **Practice... Practice... Practice... Practice... Practice...**

23. **Always be close to a smile on your face when you're practicing being kind.**

24. **Practice... Practice... Practice... Practice... Practice...**

25. **Give up as many times as you have to...and always start again.**

26. **Practice... Practice... Practice... Practice... Practice...**

27. **Practice... Practice... Practice... Practice... Practice....**

28. **Practice... Practice... Practice... Practice... Practice...**

29. **Practice... Practice... Practice... Practice... Practice...**

"Stories don't end," he says. "They just turn into new beginnings."
    ~ Lindsay Eagar from "Hour of the Bees"

APPENDIX C

Information about The Feldenkrais Method

The Feldenkrais Method

www.uncommonsensing.com

https://feldenkrais.com/

The Feldenkrais Method® uses gentle movement and directed attention to help people learn new and effective ways of moving in the world. This extraordinary method was developed by Dr. Moshe Feldenkrais. He was a physicist, engineer, mathematician and one of the first Westerners to recieve a black belt in Judo. I was fortunate to study with Dr. Feldenkrais, a true renaissance thinker, when he held his last training from 1980-1983.

Dr. Feldenkrais suffered from chronic knee injuries that he acquired when he was an avid soccer player as a young man. His life took a different direction when he was faced with serious knee surgery and he wanted an alternative to the surgery which only offered a 50% of being able to walk again. He decided to apply the knowledge he gained from his study of physics, engineering, and martial arts to a self-inquiry of his own movement habits instead of having the surgery. *The Feldenkrais Method®* was born out of this decision and his intensive self-study.

Additionally, Dr. Feldenkrais' understanding of the brain's inherent capacity to learn and develop made him one of the pioneers of neuroplasticity, long before the term came into being. His background led to this understanding and gave him a comprehension of how systems work; with this knowledge he looked at the body holistically, and created a method that re-organizes the connections between body and brain.

The Feldenkrais Method® helps people get out of pain and improve their neurological functioning and guides them to more effectively fulfill their intentions and expand their self-image.

The Feldenkrais Method® helps people move beyond physical pain, improves their neurological functioning, and guides them to effectively fulfill their intentions and expand their self-image.

Improvements in how one moves has the ability to enhance one's thinking, improve one's emotional well-being, and increase one's problem-solving ability. This is possible because the principle of systemic connection tells us everything is interrelated. If we shift one thing, we influence the rest.

Norman Doidge makes this point in his book, *The Brain's Way of Healing (Viking Press, 2015)*:

> "No part of the body can be moved without all the others being affected, Feldenkrais wrote. This holistic insight would later distinguish his approach from other forms of bodywork. Since the bones, the muscles, and the connective tissue form a whole, it is impossible to move one part, however slightly, and not influence all the others."

This is a tremendously empowering approach to the body and healing.

APPENDIX D

The five stages of learning from The Current Relevance of Merleau-Ponty's Phenomenology of Embodiment

The Current Relevance of Merleau-Ponty's Phenomenology of Embodiment

Hubert L. Dreyfus

University of California - Berkeley
Complete article at:

http://ejap.louisiana.edu/EJAP/1996.spring/dreyfus.1996.spring.html

[PARTIAL]

Stage 1: Novice

Normally, the instruction process begins with the instructor decomposing the task environment into context-free features which the beginner can recognize without benefit of experience in the task domain. The beginner is then given rules for determining actions on the basis of these features, like a computer following a program.

For purposes of illustration, let us consider two variations: a bodily or motor skill and an intellectual skill. The student automobile driver learns to recognize such interpretation-free features as speed (indicated by his speedometer) and he is given rules such as shift to second when the speedometer needle points to ten miles an hour.

The novice chess player learns a numerical value for each type of piece regardless of its position, and the rule: "Always exchange if the total value of pieces captured exceeds the value of pieces lost." He also learns when no advantageous exchanges can be found, center control should be sought, and he is given a rule defining center squares and one for calculating extent of control. Most beginners are notoriously slow players, as they attempt to remember all these rules and their priorities.

Stage 2: Advanced beginner

As the novice gains experience actually coping with real situations, he begins to note, or an instructor points out, perspicuous examples of meaningful additional aspects of the situation. After seeing a sufficient number of examples, the student learns to recognize them. Instructional maxims now can refer to these new situational aspects, recognized on the basis of experience, as well as to the objectively defined non-situational features recognizable by the novice.

The advanced beginner driver uses (situational) engine sounds as well as (non-situational) speed in his gear-shifting rules. He shifts when the motor sounds like it is straining. He learns to observe the demeanor as well as position and velocity of pedestrians or other drivers. He can, for example, distinguish the behavior of the distracted or drunken driver from of the impatient but alert one. No number of words can take the place of a few choice examples in learning these distinctions. Engine sounds cannot be adequately captured by words, and no list of objective facts enables one to predict the behavior of a pedestrian in a crosswalk as well as can the driver who has observed many pedestrians crossing streets under a variety of conditions.

With experience, the chess beginner learns to recognize over-extended positions and how to avoid them. Similarly, he begins to recognize such situational aspects of positions as a weakened king's side or a strong pawn structure despite the lack of precise and universally valid definitional rules.

Stage 3: Competence

With more experience, the number of potentially relevant elements of a real-world situation the learner is able to recognize becomes overwhelming. At this point, since a sense of what is important in any particular situation is missing, performance becomes nerve-wracking and exhausting, and the student might wonder how anybody ever masters the skill.

To cope with this problem and to achieve competence, people learn, through instruction or experience, to adopt a hierarchical perspective. First they must devise a plan, or choose a perspective, then determines which elements of the situation are to be treated as important and which ones can be ignored. By restricting themselves to only a few of the vast number of possibly relevant features and aspects, decision-making becomes easier.

The competent performer thus seeks new rules and reasoning procedures to decide upon a plan or perspective. But these rules are not as easily come by as the rules given beginners in texts and lectures. The problem is there are a vast number of different situations the learner may encounter, many differing from each other in subtle, nuanced, ways. There are, in fact, more situations than can be named or precisely defined so no one can prepare for the learner a list of what to do in each possible situation. Competent performers, therefore, have to decide for themselves what plan to choose without being sure it will be appropriate in the particular situation.

Now, coping becomes frightening rather than exhausting, and the learner feels great responsibility for his or her actions. Prior to this stage, if the learned rules didn't work out, the performer could rationalize he or she hadn't been given good enough rules rather than feel remorse because of a mistake. Now the learner feels responsible for disasters. Of course, often, at this stage, things work out well, and

a kind of relation unknown to the beginner is experienced, so learners find themselves on an emotional roller coaster.

A competent driver leaving the freeway on a curved off-ramp, after taking into account speed, surface condition, criticality of time, etc., may decide he is going too fast. He then has to decide whether to let up on the accelerator, remove his foot altogether, or step on the brake. He is relieved when he gets through the curve without mishap and shaken if he begins to go into a skid.

The class A chess player, here classed as competent, may decide after studying a position his opponent has weakened his king's defenses so an attack against the king is a viable goal. If the attack is chosen, features involving weaknesses in his own position created by the attack are ignored as are losses of pieces not essential to the attack. Removal of pieces defending the enemy king becomes salient. Successful plans induce euphoria, while mistakes are felt in the pit of the stomach.

As the competent performer become more and more emotionally involved in his or her tasks, it becomes increasingly difficult to draw back and to adopt the detached rule-following stance of the beginner. While it might seem this involvement-caused interference with detached rule-testing and improving would inhibit further skill development, in fact just the opposite seems to be the case. As we shall soon see, if the detached rule-following stance of the novice and advanced beginner is replaced by involvement, one is set for further advancement, while resistance to the frightening acceptance of risk and responsibility can lead to stagnation and ultimately to boredom and regression.

Stage 4: Proficient

Suppose events are experienced with involvement as the learner practices his skill, and , as the result of both positive and negative experiences, responses are either strengthened or inhibited. Should this happen, the performer's theory of the skill, as represented by rules and principles will gradually be replaced by situational discriminations accompanied by associated responses. Proficiency seems to develop if, and only if, experience is assimilated in this atheoretical way and intuitive behavior replaces reasoned responses.

As the brain of the performer acquires the ability to discriminate between a variety of situations entered into with concern and involvement, plans are intuitively evoked and certain aspects stand out as important without the learner standing back and choosing those plans or deciding to adopt perspective. Action becomes easier and less stressful as the learner simply sees what needs to be achieved rather than deciding, by a calculative procedure, which of several possible alternatives should be selected. There is less doubt what one is trying to accomplish is appropriate when the goal is simply obvious rather than the winner of a complex competition. In fact, at the moment of involved intuitive response there can be no doubt, since doubt comes only with detached evaluation of performance.

Remember the involved, experienced performer sees goals and salient facts, but not what to do to achieve these goals. This is inevitable since there are far fewer ways of seeing what is going on than there are ways of responding. The proficient performer simply has not yet had enough experience with the wide variety of possible responses to each of the situations he or she can now discriminate to have rendered the best response automatic. For this reason, the proficient performer, seeing the goal and the important features of the situation, must still decide what to do. To decide, he falls back on detached, rule-based determination of actions.

The proficient driver, approaching a curve on a rainy day, may intuitively know he is going dangerously fast. He then consciously decides whether to apply the brakes or merely to reduce pressure by some selected amount on the accelerator. Valuable moments may be lost while a decision is consciously chosen, or time pressure may lead to a less than optimal choice. But this driver is certainly more likely to negotiate the curve safely than the competent driver who spends additional time deciding based on speed, angle of curvature, and felt gravitational forces, the car's speed is excessive.

The proficient chess player, who is classed a master, can recognize a large repertoire of types of positions. Recognizing almost immediately and without conscious effort the sense of a position, he sets about calculating the move best achieves his goal. He may, for example, know he should attack, but he must deliberate about how best to do so.

Stage 5: Expertise

The proficient performer, immersed in the world of his skillful activity, sees what needs to be done, but decides how to do it. The expert not only knows what needs to be achieved, based on mature and practiced situational discrimination, but also knows how to achieve the goal. A more subtle and refined discrimination ability is what distinguishes the expert from the proficient performer, with further discrimination among situations all seen as similar with respect to plan or perspective distinguishing those situations requiring one action from those demanding another. With enough experience with a variety of situations, all seen from the same perspective but requiring different tactical decisions, the proficient performer gradually decomposes this class of situations into subclasses, each of which share the same decision, single action, or tactic.

This allows the immediate intuitive response to each situation which is characteristic of expertise.

The expert chess player, classed as an international master or grandmaster experiences a compelling sense of the issue and the best move. Excellent chess players can play at the rate of 5-10 seconds a move and even faster without any serious degradation in performance. At this speed they must depend almost entirely on intuition and hardly at all on analysis and comparison of alternatives. For such expert performance, the number of classes of discriminable situations, built up on the basis of experience, must be immense. It has been estimated a master chess player can distinguish roughly 50,000 types of positions.

A few years ago, my brother and I performed an experiment in which a former international junior champion, Julio Kaplan, was required to add numbers presented to him at the rate of about one number per second as rapidly as he could while at the same time playing five-second-a-move chess against a slightly weaker, but master level, player. Even with his analytical mind almost completely occupied by adding numbers, Kaplan more than held his own against the master in a series of games. Deprived of the time necessary to see problems or construct plans, Kaplan still produced fluid and coordinated, long-range strategic play.

APPENDIX E

Notes

INTRODUCTION

1. UCLA Newsroom, http://newsroom.ucla.edu/releases/ucla-bedari-kindness-institute-humane-societies, 12/18/20

CHAPTER ONE

1. Paul Bloom and Karen Wynn, "The Moral of Babies," *The New York Times Magazine,* (May 5, 2010)

CHAPTER TWO

1. Kelli Harding, MD, MPH, *The Rabbits Effect-Live Longer, Happier and Healthier with the Groundbreaking Science of Kindness,* (ATRIA Books, 2019), p. xxiii-xxv

2. Prescott Lecky, *Self-consistency: A Theory of Personality,* (Island Press, 1951), p. 169

3. Moshe Feldenkrais, *Awareness Through Movement: Easy-to-Do Health Exercises to Improve Your Posture, Vision, Imagination, and Personal Awareness,* (Harper and Row, 1972), p. 10

CHAPTER THREE

1. Attribution: https://www.sparknotes.com/psychology/psych101/socialpsychology/section3/, 12/18/20.

2. Paul Harvey, PhD, and Mark J. Martinko, PhD, *Organizational Behavior in Health Care, 2nd edition,* (Jones and Bartlett Learning: Boston, 2015), p. 147

3. Marshall Rosenberg, *Non-Violent Communication: A Language of Life,* (PuddleDancer Press, 2003), p. 41

4. Wikipedia: https://en.wikipedia.org/wiki/Spelling_of_Shakespeare%27s_name#Other_spellings, 12/18/20

5. Lavinia Plonka, *Walking Your Talk: Changing Your Life through the Magic of Body Language* (Penguin Group, 2007)

CHAPTER FOUR

1. "Self-Compassion, Self-Esteem, and Well-Being," *Social and Personality Psychology Compass*, 2011, Vol.5, No.1, 1-12, Abstract p. 1

2. Kristin D. Neff, "The Chemicals of Care: How Self-Compassion Manifests in our Bodies," https://self-compassion.org/the-chemicals-of-care-how-self-compassion-manifests-in-our-bodies/, 12/18/20

3. Joanne V. Wood, W.Q. Elaine Perunovic and John W. Lee, "Positive Self-Statements Power for Some, Peril for Others," *Psychological Science*, Vol. 20, No. 7, (July 2009), p. 860.

4. Kristin D. Neff, "The Role of Self-Compassion in Development: A Healthier Way to Relate to Oneself," *Human Development* (2009), p. 213

CHAPTER FIVE

1. Kristin D. Neff, Stephanie S. Rude, Kristin L. Kirkpatrick, "An Examination of Self-Compassion in relations to positive psychological functioning and personality traits," *Journal of Research in Personality*, 41 (4) 908-916, (August 2007), p. 909.

2. Kristin D. Neff, (2008) "Self-compassion: Moving beyond the pitfalls of a separate self-concept." In J. Bauer & H. A. Wayment (Eds.) *Transcending Self-Interest: Psychological Explorations of the Quiet Ego* (Washington DC: APA Books, 2008), p. 95-105.

3. Hubert Dreyfus, "The Current Relevance of Merleau-Ponty's Phenomenology of Embodiment," *(The Electronic Journal of Analytic Philosophy,* 4, Spring 1996,) p. 3

CHAPTER SIX

1. M.L. Terry and M.R. Leary, "Self-compassion, self-regulation, and health," *Self and Identity, Journal 10,* (May 2011), p. 3

CHAPTER EIGHT

1. Epley and Schroeder, "Mistakenly Seeking Solitude," *Journal of Experimental Psychology* (2014), p. 5 & 7.

2. Baumeister and Leary, "The Need to Belong: Desire for Interpersonal Attachments as Fundamental Human Motivation," *Psychological Bulletin* 117 (June 1995), 520 & 523.

3. In "Relationship Satisfaction among South Asian Canadians," *Interpersona Vol. 2, No. 2* (2008), Saunia Ahmad & David W. Reid reference F. K. Doell & D. W. Reid, "Partners' listening styles and relationship satisfaction: The role of listening to understand vs. listening to respond," presented at the 11th International Conference on Personal Relationships, Halifax, Nova Scotia, Canada, July 2002. P. 135

CHAPTER NINE

1. Ovul Sezer, Kelly Nault, and Nadav Klein, "Don't Underestimate the Power of Kindness at Work," *The Harvard Business Review* (May 2021)

2. J. V. Wood, S. A. Heimpel, L.A. Manwell and E. J. Whittington, "This Mood is Familiar and I Don't Deserve to Feel Better Anyway: Mechanisms Underlying Self-Esteem Differences in Motivation to Repair Sad Moods," *Journal of Personality and Social Psychology,* 96, (Feb 2009).

CHAPTER TEN

1. Paul Gilbert, *Compassion Focused Therapy: Distinctive Features* (Routledge, 2010)

CHAPTER ELEVEN

1. Kristin D. Neff and Christopher K. Germer, "A Pilot Study and Randomized Controlled Trial of the Mindful Self-Compassion Program," *Journal of Clinical Psychology* (January 2013), p. 1

2. *Powers of Ten.* https://www.youtube.com/watch?v=0fKBhvDjuy0 12/18/20

3. Phillip and Phyllis Morrison and the Office of Charles and Ray Eames, *Powers of Ten: A Book About the Relative Size of Things in the Universe and the Effect of Adding another Zero* (Scientific American Library, 1982, 1994).

CHAPTER TWELVE

1. See "Transmission and Realization," https://en.wikipedia.org/wiki/Tibetan_Buddhism, 12/18/20

2. Sharon Salzburg, Lovingkindness: *The Revolutionary Art of Happiness* (Shambhala, 2002),

3. Hutcherson CA, Seppala EM, and Gross JJ, "Loving-Kindness Meditation Increases Social Connectedness," *Emotion, 8,*, (Oct 2008). p. 720-724

4. Hutcherson CA, Seppala EM, and Gross JJ, "Loving-Kindness Meditation Increases Social Connectedness" *Emotion, 8,* (Oct 2008). p. 720-724

ACKNOWLEDGEMENTS

There are so many people who have helped me throughout this journey. Too many to mention all of them here. If you participated in this process, I am sure you know who you are. Know that I am profoundly grateful for your support, insights and encouragement.

There are a few people who I want to acknowledge specifically:

JoAnne O'Brien-Levin helped guide me toward the overall structure of this book and helped me clarify so many details. JoAnne, you were a delight to work with.
writetowisdom.com

Heloise Jones me a great deal about writing, how to understand the best ways to guide readers through the book and how to guide the reader through the exercises. In places where I didn't express things clearly, she was able to capture my voice when she rewrote sections… quite a talent! Heloise, I will always be grateful for your insights and encouragement.
https://www.heloisejones.com/

Bonita Osley's editing talent, skills and acumen brought all the finishing touches to my manuscript. She brings clarity and meaning to each sentence, each paragraph and each page. Working with Bonita is like having a conversation with an old friend, honest, direct and clear. I was so grateful to have found her… she was just what I needed.
bonita.osley@yahoo.com

Audrey Derrell, https://www.audreyderell.com/, for her wonderful photo of me.

Daniela Nakagawa, d_delamora@posteo.net, for all the help in researching (and finding!) articles and references… you went beyond my expectations.

Great thanks to Bob Lyons for his amazing cover and illustrations that communicate the essential ideas I wrote about. He helped shape this book into what it now is! Bob, you are a wonderful friend with amazing talent.

Thank you to all of you who have given me the chance to practice kindness (both successfully and unsuccessfully). Thank you for your forbearance in letting me practice and learn, letting me make mistakes with the subsequent discoveries and helping me to continue to (hopefully) become better and better at being kinder. I am still learning.

ABOUT THE AUTHOR

Alan Questel is known for his clarity, creativity and down to earth style of teaching. He brings a depth of understanding, humor and gentle human perspective while creating lively conditions for learning. Alan has taught thousands of people in over 20 countries, on 5 continents.

Trained by Dr. Feldenkrais (Amherst 1983) he has created numerous Feldenkrais programs on varied topics including one for pregnant women (Pregnant Pauses). He is author of Creating Creativity – Embodying the Creative Process.

He is still discovering how to be kinder to others and toward himself.

Manufactured by Amazon.ca
Bolton, ON